Praise for *Don't Suck, Don't Die*

"*Don't Suck, Don't Die* is not [...]
year, it's one of the most be[...]
ten. Hersh is as stunningly t[...]
sician, and her portrayal of [...]
—Michael Shaub, NPR's Best Books of 2015

"Hersh's language is vivid and conversational, as descriptive and elliptical as her own music." —*Salon*

"In under 200 little pages, it paints a more honest, insightful picture of the late singer-songwriter that any biography could. . . . Beautifully, poetically told." —*MOJO*

"A powerful and moving insight. . . . A book that will move anyone who's loved and lost, regardless of whether they're a fan of the author or of Chesnutt." —*R2*

"The book's great sadness is matched by the skill and vitality of Hersh's writing; it will make treasured and troubled reading for fans of Chesnutt and the author alike."
—*Kirkus Reviews*

"An ode, an elegy, and an examination of the physics of friendship." —WABE 90.1 Atlanta

"Through beautifully phrased, dark, honest prose, [Hersh] paints a poetic portrait of earnest struggle, friendship as significant savior, and learned empathy." —*Austin Chronicle*

DON'T SUCK, DON'T DIE

AMERICAN MUSIC SERIES
PETER BLACKSTOCK AND
DAVID MENCONI,
EDITORS

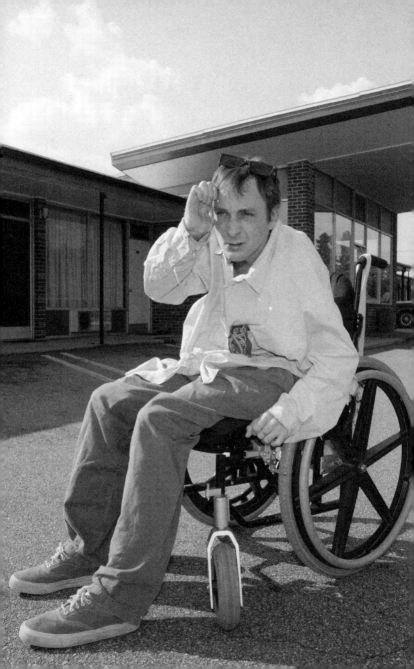

DON'T SUCK, DON'T DIE

GIVING UP VIC CHESNUTT

KRISTIN HERSH

FOREWORD BY
AMANDA PETRUSICH

UNIVERSITY OF TEXAS PRESS
AUSTIN

Requests for permission to reproduce material
from this work should be sent to:

    Permissions
    University of Texas Press
    P.O. Box 7819
    Austin, TX 78713-7819
    http://utpress.utexas.edu/index.php/rp-form

The paper used in this book meets the minimum requirements
of ANSI/NISO z39.48-1992 (R1997) (Permanence of Paper). ∞

Library of Congress Cataloging-in-Publication Data
Hersh, Kristin, author.
    Don't suck, don't die : giving up Vic Chesnutt / Kristin Hersh ;
foreword by Amanda Petrusich.
        pages   cm — (American music series)
    ISBN 978-1-4773-1136-3 (pbk : alkaline paper)
1. Chesnutt, Vic—Anecdotes. 2. Hersh, Kristin—Anecdotes.
I. Petrusich, Amanda, writer of supplementary textual content.
II. Title. III. Series: American music series (Austin, Tex.)
    ML420.C4727H47 2015
    782.42164092—dc23
    [B]   2015009516

Frontispiece: Vic in Athens, Georgia, 1996. Photo by Carl Martin.

doi:10.7560/759473

FOR TINA CHESNUTT AND BILLY O'CONNELL

CONTENTS

Vic with one of his paintings, 1988.
Photo by Rick Hawkins.

FOREWORD

AMANDA PETRUSICH

If the 1990s had a reigning ethos, it was apathy—or at least that was the party line repeated by the press, trotted out again and again to describe the supposedly listless temperament of the decade's youth. It was presumed that everyone born into Generation X was combative but disengaged, a slacker-malcontent with an armoire full of flannel and a blank stare. The soundtrack was apropos: there was the icy disaffection of Sonic Youth, the existential whine of Nirvana, the mumbled, indolent refrains of Beck.

And then there was Vic Chesnutt: feeling everything, pawing at an acoustic guitar, singing the kinds of songs that made you want to cover your mouth with your hands, they were that honest.

Vic Chesnutt was born on November 12, 1964, in Jacksonville, Florida, and was reared about three hundred miles north, in Zebulon, Georgia, where he moved with his adoptive parents as a boy. By all accounts, Chesnutt was a funny and occasionally desperate kid, and he flourished under the gentle tutelage of his grandfather, a country singer and guitarist who introduced Chesnutt to the more nourishing qualities of music. In 1983, at age eighteen, Chesnutt was in a brutal single-car accident—he'd been driving drunk, he later said—that left him almost entirely paralyzed from the neck down, although he did eventually regain limited use of his arms and hands, enough to hit a crucial handful of chords on a guitar.

In 1985, Chesnutt relocated to Athens, Georgia, the tiny university town that nurtured so-called college-rock titans like R.E.M., Neutral Milk Hotel, Elf Power, and the B-52s. There, Chesnutt met Michael Stipe, an early champion of his songwriting; Stipe ultimately produced Chesnutt's debut record, *Little*, which was released by Texas Hotel Records in 1990. "Speed Racer," one of that album's most beloved songs, showcased Chesnutt's atheism, the tenets of which would pervade his lyrics for the next twenty-five years: "I'm not a victim / I am an atheist," Chesnutt wailed over a few strummed chords. Then an electric guitar riff appeared, as if piped in from a malfunctioning AM radio in another room.

For sixteen more albums and EPs, Chesnutt sang in a crooked, southern way about darkness and pain. Jon Pareles, writing in the *New York Times*, said that Chesnutt's songs were about the "inevitability of collapse and decay," and there is a sense, listening to him sing, that his primary creative prerogative was to remind his listeners that we are all rotting away, every single moment that we are alive, and the whole of human existence is merely a long, ridiculous creep toward the same stupid end. When he was performing, he had the comportment of a person who had looked—and I mean really looked—into some kind of void. Who gets access to that vantage, and why, is an impossible thing to reason out, but proximity to that type of darkness changes a person. There was a slackness in his eyes sometimes, a droop that betrayed a truth no one wanted to see or believe: it doesn't matter if I live or die, it said, and—there was that glint, the puckish flash—it doesn't matter if you do, either. It's reductive to attribute Chesnutt's particular anguish to his paralysis (he'd exhibited signs of severe depression before the crash, and attempted suicide as a teenager), but his immobility made that pain outwardly palpable. It almost—and this is a hideous thought—felt justified, like he'd earned it. Of course, the people who loved him bucked that idea, violently.

Chesnutt spent a good chunk of the mid-1990s traveling the globe with Kristin Hersh, the front woman of the rock band Throwing Muses, as the opening act on her solo tours. Hersh was born in Atlanta to a pair of hippie parents (her grandparents, meanwhile, were strict southern Baptists) and was raised in Rhode Island; like Chesnutt, there is something unmistakably southern about her work, something cracked and bluntly soulful. In 1995, *Rolling Stone* called Throwing Muses "one of alternative rock's most influential but underappreciated groups," but by 1997 Hersh had settled into a solo career and was exploring an array of creative options, playing everything from Appalachian folk ballads to lead guitar in the aggro power trio 50 Foot Wave.

Early on in this extraordinary book, Hersh's memoir of her time with Chesnutt, there's a scene in which she smashes a bag of cinnamon candy onto Chesnutt's windshield, and what seems like an amiable road gag becomes an extended metaphor for her furious attempts to get Chesnutt to recognize, if not embrace, the tremendous sweetness of being. It's right here, she tells him, over and over and over again. It's right here. She does this work ferociously, and with the wild and propulsive tyranny of someone who knows that she is doing an important and difficult job. "Grab sugar wherever it falls" is how she first puts the idea to him. (Moments later, he tells her that it's "the gayest thing" she's ever said.)

The exchange reminds me—in its purity and vigor—of the way we sometimes try too hard to get the wrong people to love us, and how their reluctance only makes that desire deeper and more urgent. "You can't imagine how good this will be" is all we can think in that hot, panicked moment, and so we plead: "Just try it. Just try me." But fear of sweetness, fear of life—it's such an impossible thing to conceive of when you're standing on the other side of it. Chesnutt wore his disavowal of it proudly, like a medal. "I, I, I, I, I am a coward," he hollered in "Coward," a spare, arresting track from his penultimate LP, *At the Cut*. He was not an easy person to love, or be loved by, but he and Hersh seemed to recognize something in each other—maybe a shared impulse to articulate something true about the world, maybe a shared sense of being lost in it.

And so it turns out that Kristin Hersh and Vic Chesnutt were the exact right people for each other, at least for a while. This book explores that deep and devastating relationship, the oddball camaraderie of two independent-minded songwriters working at the margins of popular music. Hersh's remembrance of their tours together proffers insight into many things (music, marriage, mental illness, love, big ideas about home and the passage of time), but this book is concerned mostly with friendship. These types of heavy platonic alliances, the ones uncomplicated by sex or romance—they don't get nearly enough airplay. They can be as formative and influential as the great loves.

Sometimes it's hard to tell the difference, especially from the outside. Hersh and Chesnutt had to explain themselves a lot. In 2007, Chesnutt, in the midst of a tour for *North Star Deserter*, performed a Tiny Desk Concert for NPR, playing a mini-set of five songs, including "Very Friendly Lighthouses," which he introduced by saying, "This is not about her [Hersh], okay?" Hersh, meanwhile, tells one story about a fan approaching her and Chesnutt after a show, jubilant that he'd won a bet that she and Chesnutt were married. "Naw, we ain't married," Chesnutt replied. "She's married to a *real* man."

And there is plenty here about their respective marriages: Hersh's to her manager, Billy O'Connell, and Chesnutt's to the sweet-faced bass player Tina Whatley. It is generous to describe Chesnutt as impish and playful, and perhaps more accurate to describe him as an asshole ("I ain't got time for the niceties / Or rather I was never, never fond of the niceties," he once sang), but there was a funny kind of harmony to their hodgepodge quartet: Billy and Kristin, easy and in love; Vic and Tina, hard and in love. Marriage is trying, Hersh acknowledges, but it can be transcendent, too. ("Broken people marry *real* people," Chesnutt tells Hersh. "So they can fix us.") Nowhere do those notions come into focus faster than while suffering all the indignities of cheap and endless tour travel, hardships only ever tempered—and then briefly—by the strange ecstasy of live performance.

Night after night, Chesnutt wheeled himself out on stage, a guitar tucked into his lap, secured across his shoulders by a fraying length of string. He was almost always wearing a hat of some design: a knit beanie, an oversize newsboy cap, a straw fedora, a fake crown. His clothes were a little too big for him—the way very old men continue to wear pants that are no longer supported by their hip bones, now cinched tight at the waist with leather belts—and his face was jowly and placid, like a hound dog's. No one wants to make too much of the wheelchair, but it seems important not to make too little of it, either; there is not another artist, before or since, who has done comparable work with a comparable disability. By the mid-1990s, Hersh was also performing mostly with an acoustic guitar, playing immediate, fragile folk songs, which she sang in her tough but trembling voice. I never got to see them play together, but I imagine that the people who did still talk about those shows in hushed and reverent voices.

Hersh speaks directly to Chesnutt here, and this book feels nearly epistolary—a note to a lost ally. Like when you finally get forced into a conversation you didn't want to have, but instead of clamming up, you suddenly can't stop talking. The words pile up.

On December 22, 2009, Chesnutt swallowed a fistful of muscle relaxants. He died on Christmas Day, successfully— finally—ending his own life. He was forty-five years old.

His famous friends and admirers, from Michael Stipe to Patti Smith, felt the loss like a club to the back of the knees. Jeff Mangum of Neutral Milk Hotel wrote: "In 1991, I moved to Athens, Georgia, in search of God, but what I discovered instead was Vic Chesnutt. Hearing his music completely transformed the way I thought about writing songs, and I will forever be in his debt." Hersh herself wrote: "What this man was capable of was superhuman."

In that way, Chesnutt bucked the myth of the nineties: he fought, he engaged, he sang what he felt, even when no one wanted to hear it or believe it. That Kristin Hersh has made him so knowable here—so rich and so real—feels just as superhuman.

Vic at my house, 1996.
Photo by Billy O'Connell.

AUTHOR'S NOTE

Vic Chesnutt wasn't destined to enjoy the success many of his fans enjoyed. He influenced many and died too soon . . . an old story, but in this case the story of one of the best songwriters of our generation. He and I toured together on and off for about a decade or so and I'd say we were close, though nobody was ever close enough to Vic to cart him out of his valleys and push him up into the peaks where we all wished he'd just set up camp and send more songs rolling down that mountain into our waiting ears.

The car accident that left him a quadriplegic at age eighteen was probably his most gaping, obvious wound, but there were others. Vic was not gonna stick around, in other words, unless you believed his stories of Old Man Vic, parked on his porch in Athens, Georgia, with a shotgun aimed at all comers. *I* definitely believed that story, because I wanted to, and because when he was alive, he was *so* alive. I mean, every day . . . until he wasn't anymore.

K.H., Rhode Island, May 2015

Photo by Sandy Carson.

DON'T SUCK, DON'T DIE

I. EAT CANDY

Stepped out of the icy Alabama truck stop and into the searing sun, crinkling a bag of cinnamon Jolly Ranchers in my left hand and holding the door for a big ol' son of the south with my right. *No way northern winters are as cold as southern air-conditioning.*

Through the windshield, you did that squinty thing you used to do, when nobody could see your eyes, but somehow they were still shattering blue portals, letting everything in and nothing out. Nothing but a pinpoint of black hole judgment. The judgment was cold and cruel and . . . well, unnecessary, if you ask me. The blue portal thing was sort of blank, but the judgment always came through loud and clear. It made people cringe; so weird and unsettling. But I was used to it, so I just squinted back. No judgment in *my* squint. I squinted like a dog in the sun.

The son of the south dude balanced a box of hot dog and potato chips on a flat palm and stared into the parking lot wistfully. Sighed with his whole Buddha belly, squeezed lightly between suspenders, suspended over failing dunga-rees. His whole being was about suspension, actually. Fairly typical of a trucker. He was just . . . waiting. And his little pointy sneakered goat feet barely touched the ground. Big, fat hover dude.

Your driving glove on the steering wheel at three o'clock, you tried a muted version of the squint at me, but it wasn't gonna work. And anyway, your heart wasn't in it, cuz you hadn't had your awful cawfee yet. I smashed the Jolly Ranch-er bag up against the glass and smiled with all my evil teeth. "Eat candy!"

You, dull-eyed, through the glass: "What?"

I made the roll-down-the-car-window motion that hasn't made sense since the eighties and you said something I couldn't hear.

Me, dull-eyed, through the glass: "What?"

Shaking your head, you pointed at the AC. I rolled my eyes and let the Jolly Ranchers fall to my side. "Pussy. It's just sunshine."

So you leaned to your left and your elbow hummed the window down about three inches. Cuz nobody could call you a pussy and get away with it. Or else somebody who called you a pussy could get away with *anything*, I dunno. "You! Are the sunshine pussy and you know it!" you crowed. "Ain't nobody scareder of sunshine than you, Hersh." Then you got lost in syllables for a minute: "Sacreder, scareder . . . scared o' sacred sun . . ."

Me: "Stop that." My deformed lips shoved themselves into the three inches of van interior you'd allowed them.

"Sunshine is poison. But listen. Sweetness isn't something you can control. I mean, like hardly ever. You understand? It doesn't just come to you."

Stare. We'd been engaged in this candy debate for months. The whole tour, in fact. That sentence alone, I had uttered at least six times. Also this one: "Whatever gets you through the night, but you gotta do *all* of it, just in case you haven't found the right one yet. Cuz then dawn comes and it's too late."

"You said the dawn thing before."

"How many times? And you still don't listen." I held up the garish, fluorescent-orange bag to illustrate my point. Sparks of Alabama sun bounced off it onto my reflection in the window. "This here? Is a bag of control. Grab sugar wherever it falls."

"What?" Shaking your greasy head. "That is prob'ly the gayest thing you ever said."

Ignore. "Straight vodka? Only dulls, it doesn't bring anything to the table. And black instant coffee, for christ sake. It's cruel." Stare. A little duller than before even. "I think you *invented* black, instant coffee. Nobody on earth'd drink it except you. And you drink it lukewarm. God."

You leaned your elbow to the left again and the window closed about an inch.

Me, grim: "Nothing nice is necessarily gonna kick in is all I'm saying." I tore open the bag of Jolly Ranchers and jammed a fistful through the narrow opening in your window. You watched the candies fall into your lap. "A little tonic water, some cream and sugar; sometimes they're your only friends." Stare. "And eat candy, dammit."

That was all I had, really, and it wasn't exactly changing your life the way I'd thought it would. I figured all the talk of the last few weeks just needed some warming up with a visual aid. But you were staring at little red spheres of corn syrup and red dye number forty, serotonin levels hadn't spiked, and childhood memories of Halloween and Easter hadn't been triggered. No sugary spin had softened the noisy highway behind us or the smell of hogs and gasoline in the air. The son o' the south was still planted and wistful, suspended.

For me, cinnamon Jolly Ranchers brought forth a sensory-almost-overload of a particularly intense memory lane: terror and new love, shattering agony and heights of passion. It didn't say, "TERROR, NEW LOVE, SHATTERING AGONY AND HEIGHTS OF PASSION" on the bag, though; it just said, "CINNAMON" and it maybe had some flames on it. But you weren't even getting *that*, cuz you wouldn't goddamn eat the things.

Picking up your head, you stared through the windshield. That son o' the south was like, frozen. Frozen on the sidewalk in front of the van. It was weird. Lost his truck, I guess.

"Thank you," you muttered into the windshield.

When Tina appeared on that searing sidewalk—all rosy soft-ness and dark kindness, half a dozen braids brushing her shoulders, your sad instant coffee in her hand—the son of the south moved out of her way delicately. Floated a few feet to the left with his box of hot dog. His hot stare settled on you and your blank, hot windshield face, his hot hot dog glistening.

Tina, 1996.
Photo by
Carl Martin.

Me: "Your wife's here. Be nice or she won't give you that cup of awful."

You weren't always nice to that quiet woman. I could never really forgive you the unkindnesses you sometimes let fall on Tina's gentle shoulders. Maybe because I didn't understand, and maybe you weren't asking to be forgiven. Could have been between y'all and none of my business. In fact, I *know* that's true, but still . . . I was trying to keep you alive. Sugar is one way to enjoy being here, gratitude another.

Since Tina only had about half a dozen braids, though, glinting in the truck stop sun, I knew it was an okay day. She braided her hair when she was stressed out, and I'd seen her get up to about thirty little tiny stress braids. Two on a good day, her dark brown curls loose on the best days. Six was okay, though. The braid barometer was a fairly accurate one, so maybe you'd been a sweetheart this morning. That'd be nice. One step closer to heaven for Bitch Chesnutt.

You: "Go home to your husband and leave me alone." You watched the hot dog trucker with interest.

I turned to look at Billy, parked in the next spot, studying a map. He glanced up, smiled and waved, then returned to his map. "I think I will," I told you. "And I'm taking my candy with me." I tossed a fistful of Jolly Ranchers through *our* car window and Billy grabbed one off the seat, businesslike, cuz he knew the value of a woman holding sweetness in her hand. He'd taken part in the sweetness debate only in gentlemanly fashion: presenting y'all with beautiful vodka tonics and lattes, etc. He didn't smash candy onto your window. I believed in the direct approach. "Childlike," Tina called it. "Dog-like," you'd responded.

Now you and Tina both stared thoughtfully at the hover trucker, who was then joined by another trucker, holding a bag of Slim Jims and a vat o' soda. Together, they shuffled sadly away, into the bright white parking lot.

"Why won't faggots just be gay?" you asked with genuine concern.

The first time I saw you, you were standing on stage, bent over an amp and fiddling with the knobs in back, in soundcheck mode: a little uncertain, a lot frustrated. Every stage is a new terrain you gotta feel out and not all ropes can be learned, of course. Some of them balk at the suggestion, sneakily knotting themselves into your very own customized noose. We hang ourselves regularly when we're supposed to be making church happen, supposed to be floating song bodies out over the audience, supposed to morph into thick clouds of sound and back again.

And we're s'posed to time-trip. Time-trip from size 6X: young and fragile and confused, trying to work the spaceships we just got born into, to ninety: old and fragile and confused, trying to MacGyver our busted old spaceships into working parts that can, say, order a pizza over a fuzzy cell phone. Which we can't.

We're supposed to be slipping syringes of memories and their analogous chemicals into our bloodstreams and spitting out their shaky stories, supposed to be saving our own asses and the listeners' with our broken balls. You, when I said that: "Blah, blah, fucking blah." Because instead, we usually just highlighted the dumbass in all of us. "Retard Christ," as you so eloquently put it. Crucified on our freakin' mic stands.

"Well, *that* counts . . ." I tried.

You shook your head. "Just the difference between special and special."

Not having met you yet, though, I didn't know you were snide *or* magic. I watched you lean from side to side over your amp the way I do mine when it doesn't offer enough toggles, switches, and knobs to make a guitar sound good enough to give us a reason to ever have been born. *Where are all the other switches? The better ones?* Your forehead pressed itself into the silvery gray canvas, your knees buckling. I knew that posture in my own body so well, I figured we'd either get along great or hate each other.

Neither, as it turned out. You ignored me until somebody told you my last name, and then you pretended to pray to me. Both were weird; I kept my distance.

Anyway, I never saw you stand again.

The first time I saw you play, I watched snowy white wings unfold behind your wheelchair, poking out of your lumberjack plaid, as a six-year-old boy morphed into ninety-year-old man and back again. The spaceship dealie. The sound this made was . . . I'm gonna say "perfect" because you aren't around to hear me say it. Also because you played bass, lead, and rhythm in the same song, with only two fingers. Never heard anybody else do that before or since.

And poetry. I'm not even someone who uses the *word* poetry, but I'm gonna say your poetry "cascaded" because you would've loved to hear me say that. God, I cringe just typing it. But honestly, it was remarkable. The tumbling of it all.

Your rumpled self in rumpled clothes playing rumpled-up songs like you'd just grabbed them out of a corner of your bedroom and stuffed 'em into your suitcase before you left on tour. Which, I know, is basically what you did. Because Billy and I could hear your house in them, even though we hadn't been there yet. We could hear your hated and beloved books: paperbacks your junkie lumberjack friends'd make you read just to hear you whine about pretense and unfounded security. And the old, old, falling-apart hardcovers you'd rattle on about: their grasp of indecency and fortitude, our universal weakness and susceptibility to love lost and weather and societal convention. Which, miraculously, still had you by the throat somehow. Old when we were young, you remained out of time the whole time you were here.

We could hear your loose, rattling effects pedals that'd run out of batteries, which you considered a hopeless situation and so had tossed them into the corner to live with the spiders. We could hear Tina's mason jars of lentils and buck-wheat, could hear the rain on the metal roof of your porch. We could hear your banging pipes, which you also considered a hopeless situation. So did Billy and I, shaking our heads in frustration. Because if anybody called the plumber on you, you guys'd just hide when he came to the door. Even if it was *you* who called the plumber, you'd hide. We didn't know this yet, of course, but I swear, we could hear it. And that wasn't us, it was you. We weren't psychic, you were just a wicked salesman.

When you opened your battered old suitcase onstage and snatched another wrinkled, wadded-up song out of it, Billy and I could hear the tacky flowered sheets we would sleep under a hundred times in the future, could hear the okra growing in your backyard. We felt your kitchen pressing in: the room the four of us'd laugh so hard in, make each other wince, catch our breath, then laugh again. We were gonna make each other better, smarter, happier people in that kitchen. I already felt less lonely.

Cuz I could see the knick-knacks you would collect on our tours—also in the future—and the glass case you'd use to display them. Never quite the collection I expected it to be, given where we'd all go together (everywhere) and what confused us (everything). Never the treasures that would've reflected any kind of "universal weakness" or your mixed-up commie-libertarian leanings. You probly should've put Tina in charge of your treasure hunt. Still . . . the Six Million Dollar Man is pretty cool, I guess. Especially if you find him in Barcelona.

When you played, I heard the menagerie next door, the thirty-odd birds that dusty, hairsprayed woman kept inside with her and all the windows shut. Rats upon rats in her attic, Billy behind me on her stepladder, Tina behind him, my face sticking up through the hole in that wacky woman's ceiling, level with the rats. "*Back up*," I would hiss to our mates in the future. "*Go back down the ladder.*" Wolves in her backyard.

I heard southern trees dropping their leaves on your poor exposed porch. And I heard us walking to the co-op in the dark, your wheels splashing quietly through shining puddles on the sidewalk. Billy and Tina'd be murmuring up front, talking sweet sense, while you and I tried to arrange our precipices of flights of fancy of flying off cliffs into healthy thought forms that didn't sound as obnoxious as the way I'm describing them now. We were unsuccessful, obviously, but it was funny and that counts. Then we figured out all we had to do was present Billy and Tina with the puzzle pieces and suddenly a clear picture would emerge from our messy pile; our patient, bemused spouses smiling gently.

We also never learned to get pizza out of a cell phone, always fucked that up. Didn't even seem that hard, but confusion was in our sphere and out of our control, as if we caused it in others who'd then confuse *us*. The pizza people'd call you "ma'am" and me "sir" and it'd shake us up enough that we'd just pass the phone to Tina, who'd pass it to Billy.

But laughing is maybe better than clarity, I dunno. Pretty in the moment. What I wouldn't give to live in one of *those* moments. The pretty, laughing ones.

When Billy and I finally saw your house, it was as if we'd been there a hundred times before, having heard you play at least that many times. And then it all kicked in, came true, living backwards like songs make you do after allowing you a glimpse of the future, whether or not you wanted to see it. They tell you the whole future, see, and I wasn't cool with it. Who would be? It wasn't cool.

But it was okay. I guess. Peaks plus valleys equals a median okay, right? I mean, you played with those magic fingers. "Magic Fangers cost a quarter at the Motel 6!" you squawked to the bewildered crowd. "*You* git 'em freeeeeeee . . ." and dizzied the folks who were unprepared for a husky kid in a size 6X T-shirt and a fuzzy, gruff old dude to hold up a crystal ball and show them a picture of what happens next. *I* was certainly unprepared.

Grandma Vic. It was like you were sitting there knitting and chatting and patting the rocker next to you, inviting us all to have a seat. And, vague, uninterested, unsold, we'd look at our watches and glance over your shoulder for something better to do, something a little more exciting. It just seemed so fragile, what you did. Or quiet, or something else that might bore a rerun-addled attention span. Then you'd pat that empty chair again and wheedle-whine that you had a story to tell.

I got five minutes, we'd think and give you about that much time. But just as we were getting settled and feeling bigger than your quietness, some snow white wings'd appear behind your wheelchair. Spreading out ominously, they'd frame your odd posture, drawing our eyes away from those bony chicken wings of yours that were coming too fast for us to see. Then Grandma Vic, hell's pretty ugly angel'd jab us with a knitting needle, straight through our meat. Sometimes you'd aim for our hearts, sometimes for our viscera, sometimes right between the eyes, but every hit was a goddamn bull's-eye and us not even seeing it coming.

Never underestimate Bitch Chesnutt. That left of yours, my god: up and out. We didn't stand a chance because when you were good, the work was true. And by that I mean you were goddamn flying around the room, over our heads, kicking the crap out of us mole people. Stunned and wounded, we saw you suddenly as *yourself*: glistening, a murderous look on your face. That look that said, "this is what I do."

And then you achieved every songwriter's goal, cuz you made us think: I'm not alone.

Of course, "alone" is a different deal when you feel like a mutant, an alien. When you always felt this way; born on the wrong plane, in the wrong body. Born wrong, like I was; like a whole bunch of us were, really. Songs are fucking weird. You: "Songs will fuck. You. Up."

True.

So if you run across another of your species and he's got a better spin than the awkward *different* and *why?* you've been wearing on your sleeve for much of your life, well . . . you like it. It reduces your weirdness by at least fifty percent. Maybe more cuz it implies that there could be *other* aliens here.

I'm not alone.

Thanks for that.

Far from home. And it was always dark. I mean that literally: that year, it was always dark. Billy and I didn't even question the darkness, but y'all did, being new to this game. We *lived* in the dark; you guys blinked at it, staring into it, looking for something, an explanation.

Tina, grabbing my arm and pulling me aside: "Kristin? How can a woman live this way? I don't think I can do this." And I looked around as if seeing the darkness for the first time. In it was unwashed hunger, loneliness, sleep deprivation, hangovers, homesickness, bad air, danger, drunks, nutty fans, lo-o-o-o-o-ost . . . all that tour hardship which resonates so elaborately with an alien nature. And still, none of us ever lit any goddamn matches for fear of the gasoline fumes.

But really? Also? Because it was never dark *enough*.

"I am endeavoring to bring you the solace you seek, Ms. Hersh, and the work environment you crave in order to bring about theater magic tonight." The very British voice ping-ponged around the very British room, clipped and bored. I had no idea who was talking; it was a disembodied voice, speaking into an invisible microphone in the gaping, ornate blackness. Guy must've just come off a Shakespeare run or something; nobody's *that* English.

"I don't think 'theater magic' is gonna happen no matter *what* we do," I muttered.

"Never happened before," you pointed out helpfully from the wings. Tina stood silently behind you, arms folded, listening.

The voice ignored us, just kept Wizard-of-Oz-ing, bossy and echoing. "However, I would be remiss in my duties if I did not bring to your attention the conundrum at hand." He sighed loudly, which sounded like distortion in the speakers. "I am what is generally referred to as a 'lighting professional' here in the theater trade and, as such, am responsible for many and various lighting issues at play on this stage. Some of which conflict with others, but most of which concern the acts of seeing and being seen. Am I to understand that you have no interest in either taking place?"

What the fuck is wrong with this guy? I chuckled. "Correct, sir."

After a moment of silence, we could hear muffled thumping from above. I shielded my eyes and dodged a thick stream of dusty light to stare upward into darkness. From the orchestra pit, Billy called out, "She wants to be invisible!" *Thank you, Billy*. Billy could fix anything.

Again, a long, polite, British sigh into the microphone rang through the theater. "You can see my problem."

"The problem is English people," you pointed out delicately. "They actually do their jobs. You maybe can't ask 'em not to."

I leaned back to address you away from the mic. "I'm just asking him to do it in a particular *way*."

"You're asking a lighting guy to turn off the lights. That isn't a way, it's a not."

"Right." *Duh-uh*. "Take the night off, dude." Billy raced into the darkness and up a ladder to try and find the guy, talk him down from letting me be seen during my show.

You: "He's *theater*." Except you pronounced it *thee-ay-ter*. "The lights must go on."

"Okay." I leaned out of the beam. "Hey, sir? How 'bout you shine your lights directly into my eyes?"

"Say 'rig' to him," you suggested. "Lighting guys love that word."

"Rig," I added.

And you nodded. "Right on."

"But of course!" the British dude announced and I think I heard an eye-roll. Evidently, Billy had had some effect, though, because the guy was making his way down the ladder. He walked through the room to the orchestra pit, followed by my grinning husband, who gave me a down-low thumbs-up. Billy really could fix anything; it was nuts.

The four of us watched as the British guy climbed up a rickety ladder to move lights around with a long, metal pokey thing. He was dark and slight. Hard to imagine that Wizard of Oz voice emanating from his tiny frame. "Saw a English crow today," you announced. "Eatin' road kill."

"Yeah?" I scratched my nose with my guitar pick.

"Huge."

"Really." I tilted my head from side to side, out of the way of the swaying light beams. "I thought America had the big stuff."

"Me, too," said Billy. "No Smart Cars in America, just dumb ones."

"Our hats are big," you noted. The English dude nudged a light one more time, lining it up with my left eye. "And our McMansions."

"Your sandwiches are enormous," added the lighting guy, gripping the sides of the ladder as he backed down.

"We take half home," I told him, defensive. "Whole dang country's big, though. It's a geographical thing. Bigness is just our way."

The Englishman stared up at me from the floor of the orchestra pit. "Don't move your head." I froze as he ran back up to his booth at the back of the theater. Billy twisted his mouth up, unsure. A bored sigh from you.

"Gardens," said Tina.

I stayed dutifully still. "Huh?"

"They have little postage stamp gardens here," she said, amazed. "Our shower stalls are bigger than their gardens. We grow food in ours. Eating food."

"*You* grow food in *your* yard cuz you're hicks," I told her gently. "Most people don't."

One of your trademark squeals. "You're a hick, too!"

"Not anymore. No okra in *my* yard." I shifted on my stool, then remembered that I wasn't supposed to move. "Thanks to Billy. If you marry a New Yorker, you get automatically classy."

"Hicks are okay, I just don't like okra," Billy smiled. "Also, using the word 'classy' means you aren't."

"Mm-hm!" You nodded wildly. "That's true!"

I rolled my eyes. "That is not true." I tried to glare at my husband, but I couldn't see anything except light. "Marrying somebody from Georgia does make you a little hick-y, though . . . Billy."

"I have a little hickey," you murmured and Tina sputtered.

"Like, I got him to eat grits," I bragged. "Didn't I, honey?"

"I love grits," Billy agreed. "Can't get enough grits."

"He used to like New York goddamn City, but you know what?" Still frozen in the light beam, I paused for dramatic effect. "Not enough grits there."

"No grits at all," Billy complained. "That place freakin' blows."

"How is this soundcheck?" you bitched.

Me: "This is light check, I guess. Robins." Long squint: you had slits for eyes. "Apparently, our robins are the size of chickens." I closed the eye with the most laser beam shooting into it. "Or so an Englishman in blue underpants once told me while looking out my apartment window."

"Sounds saucy."

"It wasn't. And don't say 'saucy' in front of this guy; he'll get Shakespearean again." I leaned out of the dusty stream, took a breath. Billy carefully studied the effect of six light cans aimed at my eyeballs as colored lights flashed on and off around me: pink, blue, purple, blue, pink.

You shook your head. "Well, you shouldn't say 'under-pants' here cuz it means . . . wait . . . no, that's not it. Don't say 'pants' cuz here, it means *under*pants."

"It does?" I wondered how many times I'd used the word 'pants' in England. "So . . . an Englishman in blue . . . pants . . . told me—"

"But they're not," you grunted.

"What?"

"Robins just aren't as big as chickens." When you talked it sounded like robins chirping and chickens squawking. "I don't care if he was in his . . . pants or *not*, you can't just say that."

"Well, they might be." I closed the other eye, looked into the wings at you. "We haven't seen their chickens yet."

You nodded sagely. "How big is a pigeon here?"

"His underpants?" I added conspiratorially, "were doink. And also they were blue. Like, bright blue, nothing discreet like navy blue or anything." The lighting guy cleared his throat into the microphone. "And it was all he had on. President of my record company. He stayed dressed that way for hours. I didn't know where to look."

The Wizard of Oz: "Wondering, Ms. Hersh, if you'll forgive the impertinence, how light beams shining on your corneas is going to make it *dark* for you exactly?"

"She won't be able to see anything," Billy explained, calling upward while still training his gaze on my frozen face. The beams of light were fogging up my vision.

I blinked and my eyes watered. ". . . which is the comfort darkness affords me."

Then you came gliding out of the wings, smooth and plastic, stretching your torso out of your chair and twisting up and around, like you were made of rubbery goo, not solid meat like the rest of us. Immune to knitting-needle attack. One of your chicken-bone arms flailed high in the air as you slid across the stage. In this odd, Statue of Liberty pose, you hollered mightily into the air. "It will make her lost!" A deep breath. "She wants TO BE LO-O-O-O-OST!" And you disappeared into the wings on the opposite side of the stage.

Which is exactly—*exactly*—what I wanted to be.

Tina was still standing in the wings when light and sound-check were over. Now I grabbed *her* arm and pulled her aside. "You can do this," I told her. "Lost is good for us."

I don't know who took you to the Robin Hood Museum in Nottingham or who let you buy that stupid hat (Tina? Was it you?) but I don't remember you taking it off more than once for the rest of the tour. You were now the Sad Peter Pan and though it suited you, getting pissed off at an immigration official or launching another angry political rant in a soggy, feathered cap is just . . . I dunno, it looks *extry* nutty.

Which you loved, cuz you *were* extry nutty and probly still are. Honkin' in heaven cuz you finally love Jesus.

We saw English pigeons, though, and they were pretty much the right size. "Not gas guzzling, but serviceable," you said, "not smart, not dumb. You could take half home." Bending down to feed one a crumb of carrot cake, you stage-whispered so the pigeon couldn't hear, "*This shit makes me so sick. I get that vegan confection hangover. Golden fucking raisins and whatnot. Allspice or some shit. Let's see if he gets sick, too.*"

We watched the pigeon hop around, joining his friends at the base of a fountain. Green water poured down a green statue of a muscly man, splashing into the green pool beneath. Pigeons fluttered and hummed, I lost sight of the one we were watching, so you pointed him out. "There he is."

"I gotta go," I told you.

You sighed and looked down at your cake pigeon, the Sad Peter Pan hat slipping down over your forehead. "Figures."

Billy: "It's all about the light switches."

On the road, you live a life where absolutely nothing can be taken for granted and therefore, absolutely nothing can be ignored. Not on alert, exactly, just not given any reason to quit looking around, pointing things out, pokin' at stuff.

No country has yet entirely agreed with another when it comes to the design of light switches, for example. Or shower fixtures. Dirty in the dark, all us musicians. Something everybody seemed cool with except the four of us. We thought we were grown-ups. Or *could* be if we were allowed to turn on the lights and clean up our acts.

And though we were never allowed to stop going places, we couldn't go anywhere, either; incarcerated as we were under the Musicians = Vague Children Act. We got *put* places: van, plane, bus, hotel room, van again, dressing room, stage. But at least *we* were in charge of the light on stage. And the electricity.

The lightness and darkness and static electricity, the light/dark stasis, the electricity. The grime-ification, the cleansing, the cleansing grime. Shocks. This is how the road gets you lost and found, over and over and over again: *hey, I have no needs.* Which affords you a fresh opportunity for decency, for empathetic listening, compassionate alertness; for observation, for disappearing into the woodwork. That kind of noisy quiet suits a songwriter. Invisibility and interest complement each other when you have a soundtrack in your head reminding you that nothing needs to be brought to life, it all just *is* life.

"Nuh-uh," you snorted through a lopsided grin. "None of

that is true. Bullshit." We'd found an ersatz café in the lobby of the theater where we were playing and were killing time, as usual. Race, kill time, race, kill time. *You're right. A musician's life is boring and pointless.* You still insisted on drinking black, instant, awful cawfee, even though we were in England, even though the day was drizzly and the tea hot cocaine.

"Wall-flowering," I insisted.

"Wall-*de*-flowering," you muttered.

"What? Ew." I shivered. It was damp inside and out. I was damp inside and out. "That doesn't even make sense."

"Sure it does . . . fuck everything." You grinned like a chimp at the bleached blond woman who held a dirty cup and stirred luke-brown granules into tepid tap water for you. She took pity on the Sad Peter Pan, I think, what with the wheelchair and your dripping cap and your bitchy twitchiness. She half-smiled down at soggy you, but you didn't notice, just kept squawking. God, did you love a good squawk.

"What touring 'affords' you is a fresh opportunity to be a DICKHEAD, every-fuckin'-where you go!" Both of your arms flew up in the air as a kind of double exclamation point. The woman, taken aback, let your coffee cup drop a few inches, splashing luke-brown on the counter. "Otherwise, what are you runnin' away for?"

"I'm not running away. I'm running *to*." The woman took a dirty dishrag to the dirty countertop, staring. "And why on earth would you wanna be a dickhead everywhere you go?"

You shrugged and reached up for your half-full coffee. "Dickhead is real important sometimes."

"Dickhead is *not* important. There are too many of them."

"Truth is everything," you smirked. Such an annoying thing to say. You and annoying were so tight. You and annoying and squawking.

"Billy says there is no everything," I told you, knowing you'd never question a woman's husband's wisdom. "Only everythings."

"Interesting." You appeared to give this some actual thought, but I think now that you were just watching pigeons out the window, cuz a bunch of pigeons were going apeshit as they tumbled down from the marquee to the sidewalk in a flutter of pin feathers. And you loved flutters. You were hypnotized by flutters. Annoying and squawking and flutters.

"Dickhead-ness is everything-ness," you decided in your best hick-grandma, a couple fingers mimicking the floating pin feathers skipping across updrafts out the window.

I shook my head and paid the woman. She had an interesting pattern of warts across one cheek and she made no eye contact. Seemed to be thinking about something else. Or liked you better than me, like everybody did. I was comfortably invisible, you were visible with a vengeance. Don't know how you could stand it. "You are so lucky to have Tina," I sighed.

You sat in pigeony silence for a moment, then woke up nodding. "I'm a lucky dickhead," you agreed.

I knew that Billy and Tina were off doing all the work, as usual. *We suck*, I thought for the thousandth time; *musicians are such babies.* Our work is play, that's why we call it "playing."

You wheeled smoothly across the floor to a table by the rain-spattered window, watched the pigeon who got left behind fumble around the sidewalk, looking for something. "Wonder if that one's mine."

I sat down and stared at the wobbling bird through smudges on the window, wiped off a circle of condensation in order to see it better, check its vitals, as it were. "I dunno, does he look sick on vegan confection?" We watched him together. It occurred to me that pigeons *always* look a little sick.

"Sickly . . . dickly . . . prickly . . . nipply," you sing-songed.

I pointed my pointiest finger at you. "You're doing it again," and your eyebrows shot up into your hairline. "That's Tourette's syndrome."

"Tour-ette's syndrome?" Cough. "It's poetry."

"Wordplay. I'm not judging, but it's why you're always fucking swearing all the time, goddamn it."

"Boogers." Oil swirled across the top of your instant coffee and the pigeon took off.

Your bible went something like this:

"Chemicals charging through your bloodstream along the racket of your pulse make heroes and they make awkward and they make assholes and they make lovers and friends and they make cancerous cells replicate."

Which is the different one. Just a little bit of suicide, like lighting a cigarette or lighting a match in a dark room that's maybe gonna get warm and light or is maybe full of gasoline fumes so you . . . you know, explode. Along with the room.

I mean, probly not, but we like to stay awake. We like to ask questions: Should we encourage our cells? Or are they gonna eat us alive?

God, all the times you said this in so many different ways, your atheist kindness without trappings. I think it's cuz you sometimes gave a piece of your soul to people who didn't stop to admire it. I've seen you wheel off stage, your middle finger in the air. And we all give up pieces of our hearts to people who care enough to give up a piece of theirs and see what kinda parachute we can make together, then live for the *parachute*. Which was always gonna be better than us, more than the sum of its parts. . . was s'posed to help us survive the inevitable plummet.

Instead, you started with a broken heart and blamed everyone you met after that for breaking it. This didn't shut you down, though; just lent you a soft spot, helped you see into people's chests, see all the broken hearts around you. And I know you played music for those smashed muscles. Not a happy ending, but a sweet-as-pie beginning and middle.

We're all born living for those parachutes; I get your frustration. Images of ass-saving silk projected onto the backs of our poor eyelids, keeping our eyes wide open and searching, though they can only see that vivid parachute when they close. Pushes us in dreamy abandon toward the shininesses that move us. And when those bewitching elements of earth blind us with their shine then retreat/degrade/attack, we break, we get sick, we get dying. We get eat-ourselves-alive, which is so bad: *Hey, who broke my heart?*

We knew that someday, *someday* . . . some of us were gonna

fall. And spinning in the air, crashing to the ground, we'd suddenly realize the gone parachute was the best thing we ever did.

How did I know Billy would fall? I didn't.

How did I know you would fall? Easy. Everybody knew that. Even Tina. *Especially* Tina.

Maybe chemicals take the pulse ahead of time, get a reading and count how many holes this particular parachute's gonna have, can sense the danger in false security, false hope. Holey nylon isn't silk, you know?

"*Holey, holy holes,*" you sang another atheist hymn, "*hokey hallowed is hollow.*"

Which it isn't. "No, it isn't." I always defended everybody who'd ever believed in anything. To *you*, who couldn't seem to believe anything for more than a few minutes. Another pointless ongoing debate. "Believing is will. We keep our atoms in proximity to each other. The placebo effect is powerful and interesting. So is prayer. End of story."

"End of old story," you said, not unkindly, as you'd known lots of southern ladies like me who'd defended prayer bitterly until the end, when their last parachute twisted up in the descent and their organs responded in kind. "Moldy story, move on." And then very sweetly: "Move on, we're mutants. Git over it, you ain't on nobody's team."

You honestly didn't wanna see anybody hurt, didn't wanna see any of us stop breathing. And as much as musicians are in a race to the finish, it had nothing to do with that. It was just heartfelt kindness on your part. I wanna say it was gentleness, even though I know you'd make fun of me for imagining that you were sometimes gentle. "Wang, dang, doodle," you added for emphasis.

So the analogue for your will that is chemistry and cellular decisions like whether or not to instigate the process of feeding a mutation or destroying it, sets in motion a course of events worthy of your plot. Is that right? I couldn't always follow your discourse, peppered as it was with phrases like "wang, dang, doodle" and double negatives.

Mutations were important to you, anyway. I could have done without mine, but you figured yours made you fly. To me, music was hell; to you, heaven.

"Wang. Dang. Doodle."

"You're doing it again."

"I'm doodling." One side of your mouth smiled. A real smile, but only half of one. I don't even know what that expression *means*; I've never seen it on anyone else's face. Most half-smiles are just that: half a smile on half a face. But you could shine out of one side of your mouth and jab people with knitting needles on the other side. "Pushing the paint around," as you said in "Sad Peter Pan."

I think that was really how your bible read, you just didn't admit it or maybe even know it. You pushed the paint around. Buddha would've liked you. Jesus, too, whether you honked for him or not.

I watch you watch poisoned pigeons and I know you want to be dead. I know you'd rather be a ghost than a man. You said so: "I wanna be a ghost." You said this often, except you pronounced it "ghewst." I know how many tequila shots and pills it takes you to come down with a coma. And I know that whenever you wake up in a hospital, happy to see Tina's lovely, worried face, you're pissed off that all your shaky friends who live outside your head won't let you stop. That they are so greedy for your work and your self they don't care how much it hurts you to stay.

I didn't care. And it had nothing to do with that race to the finish. Well, maybe a little to do with that. Because I didn't like the idea of this planet without you; you were my first music cousin. When you came along and made gross and broken seem . . . I dunno, cooler, I guess . . . it was good for me. And Tina loved you. I could see that and I could see that it was important. You two had a silvery, swell parachute: y'all were a country with its own light switches and you made the world a better place.

So selfishly, I didn't care that you hurt. I liked that your mutations made me feel less strange, more worthy of clean sunshine and cleaner Billy. We *all* tried to keep you talking because shutting up is shutting down and we were already a little lonely, knowing how close you were to checking out. Fine line between "I'm not alone" and "someday I will be alone."

"Wang." The half-smile disappeared and you sat up unnecessarily straight. "Dang. I'll shut up."

I shook my head. "Nah . . . keep talking."

The next night, Billy carried my guitar into the theater, Tina carried yours. *We suck*, I thought again, stopping with you on the sidewalk to look at a poster. The theater marquee didn't have our names on it that night. Instead, it read, "SINDER-ELLA, The Naughty Fairy Tale."

"The fuck?" you asked, wheeling up under it.

"I dunno." I squinted at the poster through scratched plexiglass. "Oh, here we go: 'Sinderella, the naughty fairy tale,'" I read. "'An evening of chivalrous debauchery and decadent nastiness.'" Your blank stare. "Gross," I added.

Your wheels turning. The ones on your chair and the ones in your head. "I'm going to the prop room."

The prop room and dressing room turned out to be the same room, overheated and postwar crappy. Linoleum on the walls, paneling on the floor, as if the room had been put in sideways. You wore a used-looking Rastafarian wig with nylon dreadlocks on your head and the same wig plus a dildo over your crotch. Both smelled distinctly moldy. This is the only time I saw you without the soggy Robin Hood hat, for like, the whole tour.

"Codpiece," you said into the mirror, admiring your reflection, warmed by vanity lights that deeply infused the sideways room with the moldy scent of used Rasta wig. "Cod. Piece." In the queen's voice: "Would you like a piece of cod?"

We could hear Billy and Tina laughing far away, as they wound their way to the dressing room through a maze of crooked Alice in Wonderland hallways. You and I had navigated this route hours earlier, you spinning and bumping into the walls, acting retarded for the benefit of the cute girl who led us here. Now we were afraid to leave the dressing room, knew neither of us could find our way back if we did. Billy was doing his perfect impression of a British TV host for Tina as the two of them got closer.

"Y'awright?!" Billy yelled as they burst in, Tina covering her mouth with one hand and twinkling her eyes. Billy smiled at me, then immediately left the dressing room. I flushed and my stomach lurched, which is what always happened when Billy appeared or disappeared. Note to self: you don't have to be fearless, just . . . fear *less*. Don't get careless, just care *less*.

By your side was a gray, dusty prop sheep, whom you'd nicknamed "Dolly," claiming that she didn't move or breathe because she was a clone. "That's not how clones work," I said, admiring your ability to drape yourself in and surround yourself with crud; crud made you happy.

"Dolly. Dollies. Dollywood." You caught Tina's eye in the mirror, jealous that another man had made her laugh. "Why, ain't you a baby doll, baby doll . . ." But now Tina was reading a magazine, ignoring you, as usual. So you got louder. As usual. "Were all the clones named Dolly, too? How many Dollies were there, do we know?"

I shook my head, fishing around in my makeup bag. I was learning to ignore your prattling, too. So you got even louder: "Well, it was named after Dolly Parton, you know. Because of her big tits." I squinted at you. "It's true." Seating your knitted Rasta cap more firmly on your head, you swung some beaded, nylon dreadlocks over your shoulder. "They cloned a mammary gland or some such." Taking a minute to admire your reflection, you spoke into a fan whirring on the counter: "I. Am. A. Sad. Clown."

Billy burst back in, carrying an armload of beer and a plastic container full of ice. Flush/lurch. "Ice in England!" he grinned, triumphant. "Who's your favorite tour manager?"

I kissed him. "Ice in England is truly an impressive feat," I announced, in case you guys didn't know this.

You stuck your sneakers out. "Truly impressive feet."

Tina grabbed a newspaper off the stained coffee table and sat down to read it, then held it away from her face in disgust. "I can't figure out if these people are prudish or gross."

"Mammary glands," I agreed.

"They say the same thing about Americans," Billy pointed out. "They think we're prudish and gross."

"But . . . they have a queen and topless young girls." Tina grimaced, holding the paper out carefully, like it might infect her.

I glanced at it. "Ew."

She studied the image with one eye, from a few feet away. "It's amazing how invisible a woman can be until she takes her top off."

That was a seriously depressing thought.

"Everybody's invisible," Billy said comfortingly. "And prudish and gross work together." Repeat: Billy could fix *anything*.

Opening a tube of mascara, I thought about this. "I guess if their queen *was* a topless young girl, they'd be gross. But they have to maintain the prudish thing so they can fuck with it. Stuff can be 'naughty' here. We don't have naughty in America. Wish we did."

Billy: "They're compartmentalized. Like a social red light district."

I looked up at him. "A topless queen'd be cool, though. Like, if she kept her crown on and her ermine robe and held a scepter but she was nude."

"She'd be *naked* if she had all those accoutrements," he corrected.

"Right. The naked queen. For, like, charity."

"So, Dolly . . ." You didn't like being ignored.

"Or . . .," I continued, "the queen could be *nude* for charity because she doesn't need to prove what she does for a living. Cuz her face is on money, she's pretty recognizable. So, you know, it could be very tasteful." I worked the mascara brush over my eyelashes until they looked gummy and awful. "For charity."

You adjusted your codpiece with both hands. "Dolly Parton once handed me a beer."

I leaned into the mirror to rub off the mascara I'd just applied, smeared it all over my eye sockets.

"Really?" Billy turned to Tina. "Did that happen?"

"James Victor," she giggled and sighed. And to Billy, "Sorta."

"Course it happened," you growled, brushing smelly dreadlocks out of your eyes. "Dolly Parton. Dolly, pardon. Pardon Dolly, for she is but a clone. A country-singing, beer-swilling, big-titted, woolly clone." I never knew what to make of your stories. It's as if they were all *almost* true. "*She lives in Dollywood*," you sang, "*ruling as a naked queen.*"

"Nude," I corrected.

"Fucks with the meter," you grumbled, then continued your reverie: "*She rules the woods of Dolly/with hands graceful and mean.*"

Billy found tonight's deal sheet and slammed his metal tour manager case shut, ran out the door, and disappeared into the Rube Goldberg maze of hallways. I stared at the door with my black eye sockets, flushing and lurching, but just a little. Tina stared at the door, too. "He doesn't stop, does he?" I shook my head and Tina frowned. "I'll never be anyone's favorite tour manager."

"Not true," you told her sweetly.

In the mirror was a broken drag queen reflection. Me, into the whirring fan: "I. Am. A. Sad. Drag. Queen."

"*She's a sad dra-ag queen,*" you sang softly.

Giving up on the mascara, I studied you. "You should maybe not wear that tonight."

"Which?"

I said nothing, grabbed a lipstick out of my bag.

"You wear lipstick, I wear codpieces," you sighed happily. "It's a the-ay-ter thing. I'm show people."

"Makeup means I'm hiding cuz people can't see my real face. Codpieces mean they stare."

"At somebody else's weenis." I didn't respond, so you kept going, of course. "And I got a flimsy ego, so I like it when they stare. Also? Joni Mitchell once burned me with a cigarette."

"That definitely happened," Tina piped up behind me.

I whipped around. "Joni Mitchell *burned* him?"

"With a cigarette!" you added proudly, back in the spotlight.

"Why? Where?"

Grinning wildly: "Cuz she was drunk . . . on the arm."

I was still holding my lipstick, had forgotten what it was for. "Joni Mitchell burned you."

Your eyebrows shot up, pulling your dreadlocks up with them. "She leaned over and put her cigarette out *on my arm*."

"No shit."

Tina turned a page in her newspaper. "No shit."

Quickly, I smeared on some lipstick and then, shaking my head, wiped it off again. You, into the fan: "You. Are. A. Lousy. Drag. Queen." Frown. "Quit wipin' off your makeup."

"Okay." I applied more lipstick. "My mouth is on wrong, though. Lipstick just highlights my deformity." You watched my mouth in the mirror.

"Oh yeah," you stared. "You *are* deformed. Gross."

"Mm-hm." I wiped off my third attempt at lipstick. "I have to draw on different lips. Plus, look how many teeth I have."

Tina squinted up at my reflection. "Too many."

I nodded sadly.

But now you were bored, had moved on. Peering at the prop sheep's rear end, you yelled: "This clone has a HUGE vagina!"

That night, you sped onto the stage—glided, I guess—with Dolly the sheep on your lap, next to your grandfather's guitar. No one could see any part of you but your legs and Rasta hat. "See you in my dreams!" you called to Tina, as we waited in the wings, ready to watch from side of stage.

You placed Dolly carefully at your side, singing to yourself. "*Beautiful Tina, wake unto me . . . .*" Then, plunking away at those stretchy, detuned nylon strings, you began "Rabbit Box"—or maybe it was "Speed Racer"—live, I used to get those two mixed up. Somehow, the notes themselves would stretch along with your bendy strings, the way you used to stretch syllables. But as soon as this curving began to kick in, a miffed theater dude strode onstage in all his affronted glory and snatched Dolly from your side. You stopped playing and looked up at him.

"This is not your sheep!" he hissed at you, but near enough to the mic that the whole audience could hear.

I woulda been embarrassed, I think, accused of stealing a sheep clone with a huge vagina in front of hundreds of people, but not you. I don't think you *got* embarrassed. I mean, like, ever. Shame was somehow not in your emotional vocabulary. Crud made you happy, humiliation made you happy . . . so why weren't you happy?

I looked up at Billy, who just looked surprised. Tina slapped her forehead, mortified. But you? You were gleeful, as if you'd scripted the whole thing and it was coming off without a hitch. That silent, open-mouthed laugh of yours as the guy spun on his heels and took off with your sheep friend. That silent laugh that meant: win.

"I am the Victor!" you would shout sometimes, whenever there was too much silence going on, cuz your name actually meant "winner" of all things. The craziest thing—and I mean this literally—*the* craziest thing about you was that "win" always meant: lose.

A train station in Paris, the four of us debating who on earth has the dumbest accent. "We do!" I insisted and Billy nodded. "Everybody knows a southern accent drops your IQ by dozens of points," he said warmly, putting a pitying arm around my shoulders.

"No," answered Tina softly, making hick sound gentle and intelligent. "Brooklyn."

"Pretty du-umb," you agreed in your widest Gomer. Billy, who is from New York, let his jaw drop.

"Not in movies," I said quickly, glancing up at him. "Don't worry, honey, New York's *cool*."

"Don't patronize me," Billy frowned down at me suspiciously. "You hicks argue about who had the biggest hog. New York children are not hog children."

This was true. You and Tina and I had *just* been arguing about who had the biggest hog when we were kids: "He was Hogzilla! You shoulda seen 'im," etc. So yeah, we were hog children. Who'da thunk it?

An announcement about the arriving train over the loudspeaker. In French, of course. "French is pretty stupid," you said loudly enough for all the French people around us to hear.

Tina rolled her eyes. "Brooklyn," she said again and Billy shook his head sadly, feeling sorry for us southerners.

I thought for a minute. "Valley?" California seemed nice and neutral.

You shrugged, glaring at passersby racing to their trains, holding briefcases and paper cups, speaking continuously. "FRENCH!" you shouted at them all.

Flying somewhere. I remember a royal blue carpet and glass walls. No idea where we were going. Probly had no idea then, either. At the gate, I saw your eyes roll back in your head. I was alarmed. "What's the matter with *him*?"

Tina glared at you. "He took drugs in the men's room."

Wow. So rock. "What drugs?"

"We don't know," sighed Tina. "Mystery drugs."

You snapped awake. "Just one drug and I do too know. It was a goddamn methadone."

"You don't know what methadone looks like in this country," she said.

"Ex-junkies all know methadone." Your head lolled. "Found it on the bathroom floor," you explained politely, moving your lips carefully, like you had to move each one independently. "Handi-stall. Swallowing it seemed like the thing to do."

Jesus. I watched you fade into yourself, sick. Weird-ass junkie retard Christ. Sorry, *ex*-junkie. The only way you could stop suffering was to suffer some more. Billy and I looked at each other, then down at you from our clean planet, so distant from yours. Earth is such a simple plane when you don't grab the screaming brakes and pull back. I'm sorry. Even though you hated sorry, I'm still sorry.

"Seemed like the smart thing to do," you insisted. "Pain-killer," you slurred then and looked up at me. "Every hurt heals with scar tissue." You had the same expression on your face then that you had on stage every night. It said: this is what I do.

In Hamburg, you put thumbtacks on every hammer of the grand piano in the Kleine Musikhalle, playing ragtime porn for our entertainment: X-rated Scott Joplin, just bizarre. Can't imagine what the next concert pianist who sat down to play at that piano thought. We hoped that you'd infused the instrument with your passion for dirty limericks and rollicking drinking tunes, so that from now on, Tourettic sea shanties'd fly off the keys, thumbtacks clacking, sheet music floating gently to the floor, forgotten. You had a way of leaving your mark without anyone even knowing you'd done so.

Dropping my backpack on the floor of our hotel room that night, I dove onto the bed, exhausted. Lovely German beds, with those white comforters. I never wanted to leave any German bed.

It was dark in there except for moonlight and the glowing whiteness of the room itself. Billy, who worked much harder than I did at shows, dragged my guitar into the room, then fell onto the bed next to me. Finally, everything was quiet except for our ringing ears. We'd left the window open after checking in that afternoon, but, unlike in America, there was no highway outside to whine and roar at us. Only wet branches, brushing against each other in a light rain. We breathed the silence and the wetness in, listened to the semi-tones our damaged eardrums played.

"We're dirty," Billy said.

I turned to face him. "*I'm* not." There was a strip of moonlight across his eyes, like an anti-mask.

"Okay. But I'm gonna shower." He reached for the reading lamp on his bedside table. "I'm turning on the light so you don't fall asleep." *Click.* Looking up at the ceiling, I grabbed his arm before he could move. "What?" he asked, alarmed.

I couldn't find the words, just kept looking up, so he followed my gaze. A cloud of transparent insects at least a foot thick covered the entire ceiling, shifting in silent waves like a wheat field. Billy jumped. "Oh my god!"

It was amazing. "There must be billions of them."

"Trillions," he said and reached for the phone. "I'm calling the front desk."

"I took German in high school," I offered, but the desk clerk had already picked up; I could hear his crisp voice through the receiver.

"Yeah, uh, hi," Billy couldn't take his eyes off the ceiling. "I'm sorry, I don't speak German."

"That's fine," responded the clerk in English.

"I hate to disturb you. But. We just got into our room? And, well. We left the window open and a whole lot of bugs must've flown in. Because there are a whole lot of . . ." He couldn't think for staring at the roiling cloud above us, "bugs in here." Silence. "Like, a *whole* lot."

"Bugs?" asked the clerk politely.

"Insects?"

"Ah. Okay, I see." More silence. "Please hold."

Billy lay his head back down on the pillow to get a better view of the ceiling. "I'm holding," he told me.

"Whadda you expect the guy to do?" I asked him. "It's after midnight."

I heard a tinny shuffling through the receiver and the clerk cleared his throat. "You should want to know this. They don't . . ." he said and paused. "They don't . . . *peck* you."

Billy thanked him and turned off the light.

We did so love that darkness.

The end of the tour. And all those little Kinder Surprise toys wrestling for real estate on your dashboard. You'd been pitching the chocolate eggs and collecting the toys inside them the whole time we were in Europe; you had, like, hundreds. Tina said she'd set 'em all upright again every time you took a particularly violent left turn down another strasse named what the last strasse that got you lost was named.

Billy and I in our own vehicle, winding over cobblestones, past red flowers in window boxes, red graffiti on red butcher shops, dark with dark red blood: "What the hell animal did that used to be?" And shopping Germans, pressed and articulate, pulling little metal carts behind them. Tilted sunbeams shining down alleys, sparkling through truck exhaust. These are Billy's light switches: the tilting, the sparkling that kept us awake.

You squawked something about Nietzsche out the window and took another sudden left, laying waste to dozens of little plastic monkeys playing accordions and floppy, skateboarding dogs, Tina patiently re-seating them all in careful dioramas. Your favorite, I remember, was a world-class little machine that snapped together only for those with infinite patience, but paid off in spades by flying itself around the dressing room, over the heads of people who took anything too seriously. Honestly, you wouldn't just let that toy fly, you always had an ulterior motive: *show the dumbass who's a dumbass*, I guess. Your default motive. Especially if you could shoot yourself in the foot at the same time: if *you* were the dumbass. Win = lose, but lose = win.

A right turn down a strasse named something like, fifty syllables of glottal rattle, and you screeched to a halt to stop and study a map. We pulled up behind you as a little boy's head stuck out a window. He called down to nobody on the sidewalk.

Then Tina pointed out the window of your van, at a little gray cat who looked lightly up at the boy and called back to him. The boy giggled down at her and told her to wait for him. "*Auf mich warten!*" He pulled his head inside.

Tina and Billy and I were deeply charmed. She smiled an out-the-car-window smile that said: *We need the cat and the boy. This is what lost is for.*

"Damn it and fuck, got no time for lost!" you yelled.

Which was exactly—*exactly*—the difference between you and us.

Four days in Spain, Billy and I holding hands, bumping along in the backseat of a van on the way to the grounds of a summer festival that was blending with other summer festivals. Days were morphing into memories as we got further into the tour and away from our own brains. Light switch limbo: lost and found eventually degrades into just lost and you think fuzzy. You say things before and after they happen, but your mouth can't quite grasp what's happening *now*. Your brain doesn't ever have any idea what's happening *now*, either, because it's busy comparing now to some other time, here to some other place. So busy that it doesn't notice your skull cracking open around it.

Then simple, important things seem so awfully impossible. One minute, you're on a clean planet—on solid ground—and the next? On a tightrope over a yawning chasm. *What the fuck*? Light switch limbo is not a place of balance, but a war of extremes.

Fuzzy, I had more insight than I wanted. A snapshot of a truth: a complete whole, my husband was full of holes. I'd reach for Billy's arm and my world'd break down into slo-mo cuz Billy the being was . . . missing. And I missed him. Like his soul'd slipped out, a slippery slip of a safety net. I wanted so badly to help him, but I was scared.

Sometimes he was a hover heart and nothing else. Sometimes everything in the man was intact *but* his heart. Which'd been carefully removed. Who cut him open? I'll never know. But I envied him at those times. Heartless was clearly a safer way to be.

Shaking off my shaky heart, I crumpled up this snapshot and shoved it into a limbic photo album, left it on a motel nightstand in my amygdala to degrade. Just a nightmare, burning up in the light of day. Snapped out of that snapshot, I chose to forget its warning. Care less, fear less.

Our European tour with Vic and Tina over, the four of us'd said a sleepy good-bye, a pretend good-bye, a bored good-bye, because America was waiting; a huge, hungry mouth of unplayed shows. We could kill *years* touring America.

Now Billy and I had been awake for at least thirty-six hours except for dozing off on airplanes seconds before they landed; something we both do, for some reason. And Spain always felt strange and lonelifying, but particularly now. At the end of a tour, you get weak. Your body finally says, *now?* and collapses. Even if tonight you have to stand alone on a stage in front of thousands of people. I kept trying to get my brain to tell my mouth to whisper to my body that it had to keep going, but nobody was talking to anybody, so I rested my head on Billy's shoulder and stilled, watching. Half my life I spent resting my head on Billy's shoulder and watching. Holey or holy, his shoulder was the only thing that could still me.

This morning, the world was hot and dusty, and the friendly, oily, smoking guy driving the van spoke English words as if they were Spanish ones. I thought Billy was following the rising-then-dipping monologue—he laughed and nodded, then looked appropriately thoughtful—until he turned to me and shrugged. I smiled. Lonely together is the opposite of lonely. *Fuck lonely, we win.*

Enchanted by the driver's long, wavy, glistening hair as it moved around on his back, independent of its owner, I began to hear the sounds he was making not as words, but as rhythm and melody. The staccato syllables swelled in volume and changed keys, then resolved like a musical movement. When he talked, the man's cigarette sent smoke into the glistening black snake hanging off his head. The smoke then settled into a waxy coating on what looked like one big hair, like a piece of petrified wood.

When we pulled up at the festival hotel, I realized we'd both dozed off again. Dreaming of wooden-haired gnomes smoking in olive groves in the steppe country, probly. Billy opened his eyes as wide as he could, hoping they'd stay that way, and they did, just long enough for him to peer out the window and yell, "Vic!"

I stayed quiet, waiting for the rest of the sentence cuz that one word made no sense and I was missing the shoulder he'd pulled away so cruelly. I was also still in gnome country, prepping my tired muscles to lift both a suitcase and a guitar when those muscles didn't wanna budge from the vinyl bench they were parked on. "Vic!" Billy yelled again, this time for your benefit, not mine.

And dang, you were just sitting there, perfectly framed by the van window, like you'd been sent to welcome us. Squinting into the sunshine, parked with your hands folded and your sneakers crossed. Looked like you had nothing better to do than sit on a sidewalk in Barcelona at exactly the same time we had nothing better to do than crawl out of a van in Barcelona. "What's *he* doing here?"

Billy jumped out and stood next to you. "What the hell?"

You: "What the fuck?"

Him: "You weren't supposed to be here."

You: "*You* weren't supposed to be here."

The driving gnome, cigarette between his teeth, kept chattering as he tossed our belongings onto the sidewalk. I ran to the back of the van and caught my guitar in the air as it left his hands. "*Gracias!*" I smiled at him and he winked at me through smoke, his open eye watery and sparkling.

"The tour's over! Go home!" I yelled at you, holding my guitar in my arms like a baby. I stared at you. You stared back. "Where's Tina?" I asked accusingly.

"Droppin' a log."

"Nice." Billy laughed and stumbled off. "Checkin' into the hotel; be right back!"

I placed my guitar carefully on the hot sidewalk and we continued to stare at each other. Well, squint. Spanish sun is stronger than ours and we were both constitutionally challenged. Your mouth twisted up. "Got any food?"

"Nope. You?"

"Nope." You uncrossed your sneakers, then re-crossed them. Your shoelaces were outlandish: one day-glo green with cat faces on it, the other a purple and pink checkered pattern. "Water?"

"Nope."

"We're gonna die."

That afternoon, the four of us went exploring. Foraging, really, cuz we *were* gonna die if we didn't find food and water soon. Moving carefully along the sidewalk, we didn't belong, didn't belong, didn't belong. And our other-than-ness was palpable; people stared.

"But why don't we belong?" asked Tina under her breath. "I've never been able to figure that out. We're nomadic people, we wander, we should just *be* everywhere we go, period." She shook her head sadly. "But we don't belong."

"And they can all tell," I pointed out. "Everybody's staring at us."

"Man, that happens every-fucking-where," you growled. "Every fuckin', every fuckin', every fuckin' where."

Billy: "That's true."

I remembered Billy's comforting shoulder and the oily gnome. *Fuck lonely.* "But we don't belong *together*." You rolled your eyes and rolled away.

We stopped to admire a dripping Gaudí building. Looked like where I imagined that nice, greasy gnome'd live. Out in his olive grove. Full of smoke and hair oil. I was starting to fall asleep again. Or maybe pass out. I shook it off. "Know what, though? They don't stare in the midwest."

"Huh?" Tina screwed up her face. "Really? I never noticed."

"Actually, yeah," Billy nodded. "I don't know if they're too polite or what."

"It's cuz we dress like farm people," I said.

Your poor wife looked insulted. "Speak for yourself."

I studied her corduroys, work boots, old T-shirt, and flannel overshirt. Exactly what I had on. And what you and Billy were wearing. "We dress like farm people," I told her again sadly.

She sighed, looking me up and down, then stared at her own clothes, finally settling her gaze on her feet. "I guess we do." You were up the street aways, peering into a shop window suspiciously.

"And they don't stare in New Orleans," I said.

"Cuz they're all nuts," agreed Billy.

"I think it's cuz they sleep in their clothes, like us."

Tina nodded. "*If* we sleep."

"We're rumpled, either way."

You narrowly avoided running over an elderly woman dressed in black lace. She was pulling a grocery cart full of vegetables and the meaty leg bone of something. You spun and screeched to a stop like you were riding a big wheel. "LEG BO-O-O-ONE!" you scream-squealed. The lady thought you yelled this at her and she yelled something back in Spanish angrily. Again, your silent laugh that meant "win" but really: *lose*.

Fun fact: the way you said "bone," it had four syllables somehow. Usually, it only has one. *Four*. That's a lot.

When we finally found a grocery store, it was a huge warehouse that sold the Spanish version of . . . everything. And not in any particular order. Swimming trunks next to wine, next to soup, next to that leg of something the old lady in black lace was pulling in her cart, next to comic books, next to birthday candles.

Billy and I were looking for gazpacho; you and Tina wanted hummus. We wandered down aisle after aisle, naming products on shelves that weren't what we wanted. "Cakes, condoms, cereal, inner tubes," you muttered.

"Diapers," added Billy. "Hunting knives, pork, lipstick."

Tina ran her finger along the edge of a freezer. "Squid, TV dinners, fish heads."

"Cookies, tampons, board games . . . more squid," I complained.

Zooming across the linoleum, you lifted your arms over your head and flew down the aisle. "We're gonna die!"

"We should ask someone for help," Billy decided.

I looked up at him hopefully. "Do you speak Spanish now?"

He edged away, looking for a store employee. "I speak . . . pantomime." Tina looked unsure, but followed him anyway.

"How's this gonna work?" I asked her.

"I dunno," she shrugged. "I'm really hungry."

"Okay. Billy can fix anything."

She stopped and nodded, wide-eyed. "I know . . . and we can't fix *anything*."

This was, of course, the difference between Billy and *us*.

Parked at the end of the aisle with your nose in a display case, you yelled into it, "You gonna feed me, Tina?" Grimy with Spanish dust, you looked sepia-toned.

"Feed yourself!" she called back, racing after Billy. "I'm tired of babysitting you! And your giant ego!" *Yikes*. This was as close to bitterness or scolding as I'd ever heard the gentle Tina get. And it didn't get your nose outta the display case. Figuring you must've found something good, I wandered over and peered down into it. "Naked Spanish chicks," you explained.

"You guys okay?" I asked. The display case was overflowing with glossy magazines covered in tits and asses and fluorescent Spanish words. I winced and stepped back.

"I just wanna see where they shave."

"Oh." I turned my back on the naked magazines, scanning the aisles for signs of Billy fixing stuff. "So . . . you have a giant ego? I thought you had a *flimsy* ego."

"One and the same."

"Huh." Couldn't figure out why you weren't upset that Tina was mad at you. I would *die* if Billy talked to me like that. Freeze, tip over, fall down, dead. "So?"

You reached into the bin and pulled out a magazine with your thumb and driving glove. "So what?"

"Where do Spanish chicks shave?"

"*No*where."

Chuckling, I looked at you out of the corner of my eye. "And your ego's like, what, a giant . . . bubble?"

"You could pop it with one finger." Gripping the magazine and holding it over your head, you announced, "Mustaches!" Then you dropped the magazine on your lap and began turning pages. "All *over* 'em." I waited for you to be done, now that you'd figured out where the women didn't shave, but you kept turning pages. Then you sang, "*Mustaches, tits, asses, let's shave nowhere. Beautiful, beautiful, beautiful hair.*"

Caught a glimpse of Billy and Tina a few aisles over, trying to communicate with a store employee in a salmon-colored lab coat. "Well that's cool, I guess," I said, making a ponytail outta my hair to lift it off my hot neck. Spain did not shave *or* air-condition, it seemed. Better adjusted than us. "Women with hair should probly be allowed to have it, right?"

You coughed. "Are you implying that these are feminist publications?"

"Well, no. Are there naked guy magazines in there? That'd even things out a little." You peered in again with one eye, then shook your head. I shrugged. "Hairy is just a nice, easy way of being. Culturally." You kept turning pages. "Every woman should be allowed to turn every man on. And turn every lesbian on, right?"

"Hmmmm." You tossed the mustached women with enormo-tits back into the bin and studied what was happening between our spouses and the woman in the salmon lab coat. "I don't know . . ."

"Yeah, you're right," I admitted. "People gotta smell pheromonally right. And also be nice."

Billy and Tina were indeed engaging in pantomime. Because I knew what they were looking for, I knew what they were doing: pretending to grind up chickpeas. The woman looked baffled, however. Tina had actually found a can of chickpeas and was holding it up to illustrate what Billy was doing with his invisible mortar and pestle. Her grip on the can slipped, though, as she began to giggle, then laugh. The can rolled down the aisle and she chased it, still laughing.

"They are amazing," I said, with much concern. As far as I knew, that crumpled snapshot was a gone moment, banished as it was to the motel room in my amygdala, but looking at Billy still hurt. Tried to see him in the future as my broken-down house, the one I belonged in, that nobody else would even look at, but he wouldn't stop shining. Same as walking away. "Look at 'em, they're trying to *feed* us cuz we're too dumb to feed ourselves."

You were grim, too, watching your pissed-off wife laughing. "I am not turned on by every woman."

"No," I sighed. "I'm not turned on by every man." Billy took the can of garbanzo beans from Tina and began pounding it with a pantomime hammer. The store employee's eyebrows shot up.

You nodded slowly. An architected stare at our spouses and the busted hearts they held in their angry hands. I couldn't help wincing at Billy's invisible hammer. *Careful.* I thought this word to myself a lot. When I looked down at you, the words tumbled out: "Is Tina mad at you?"

"Yep."

"You guys're okay, though, right?"

"Hell, no!" you shrieked suddenly, as if you knew I was gonna ask this rather forward and girly question. "And then sometimes? Hell, yeah."

I watched you, waiting for more, but you'd said your piece, so I sighed a long, mopey sigh. Billy mimed pouring a bowl of gazpacho and eating it with a spoon as Tina held a tomato in the air helpfully.

I sighed again and you rolled your eyes. "He loves you, I can tell," you threw out, bored.

"Sometimes I think he doesn't even *like* me."

"Nobody likes you."

"Fair enough."

You: "We're never gonna be okay cuz we got fucked-up egos."

"*I* don't have a fucked-up ego," I told you, defensive. "I don't have an ego at all."

"Well, that's fucked up."

"Oh."

Pitching your magazine back in the bin, you grabbed another. "Every hurt heals with scar tissue."

"That's what you said about painkillers."

Pointing at our loved ones: "Whaddyou think *they* are?"

Oh.

The store employee stuffed her hands into her salmon pockets and relaxed, watching Billy and Tina's performance happily. We watched, too, and forgot our hunger. I noticed that their "pantomime" involved a lot of chatter. "They're better than us," I realized out loud.

"Right on," you nodded, looking over at them carelessly. "Reasons to live," you added. Note: this is a fairly weighty add-on and you didn't give it a ton of emphasis. I wish you'd listened harder when you talked.

"Glad you guys came to Barcelona," I said.

"They made us," you snorted. "We didn't come here to see you. When I said good-bye, I *meant* it. I'm sick o' you guys."

"Yeah. We're sick o' you, too. But it's usually lonelifying here." I grabbed a dirty magazine out of the bin and studied the glossy, tanned skin and fluorescent letters. Tossed it back in with the others. "Now it's not."

You smirked and spun around. "Cuz we don't belong." Tina and Billy and the woman were now all laughing and we were no closer to eating. Then you bothered to repeat my stupid truism that made everything okay, even though you did it in a high squeaky puppet voice, imitating my low, husky man voice: "But we don't belong *together*."

II. THICKETY TIME

Back in Alabama, we watched those two sons of the south amble over to their trucks in the glaring sun, cardboard box o' hot dogs and Slim Jims in hand. You opened one of the cinnamon Jolly Ranchers, of all things, but you didn't put it in your mouth; just used the wrapper to wave off a fly.

"*Please don't say 'faggot' any louder than you just did,*" I hissed through the cracked window of the van.

Lowering the window another few inches, you squawked, "I loves me some faggots! You know I do!" I whipped my head around to see if the truckers had heard, but they were still walking quietly across the parking lot. Yelling now: "Me and the gays are tight! Tight as can be, almost! 'Cept for the sodomy part!"

Christ.

"Republican sons-uh-bitches!" you tried, but couldn't get a rise out of 'em, couldn't even get 'em to turn around.

"You know," I complained, "it's not the *wheelchair guy* who's gonna get the shit kicked out of him. It's his *friends*."

Tina, patient as always, not really listening actually, let the fly out her window. I watched as you crumpled up the candy wrapper and shoved the Jolly Rancher into your mouth. *Phew*. A little sugar for Vic today. "Thank you."

"Fuck you," you muttered, dismissing me, then rolled your window all the way down and careened your van past the sons of the south.

Oh shit.

"Morning, gentlemen!" you called to them and waved. They waved back mildly, had trouble lifting their arms, loaded as they were with trucker chow. But your chicken arm kept going; a long, slow wave as you and Tina disappeared down another highway.

"God, I love cheap motels." I fingered a plastic flower on a plastic coffee table.

You moved your tongue around inside your mouth, trying to find a melody. No fucking barrier between your brain and your tongue, I swear. "*Gawd, how I love me the cheapest motel,*" you sang. Anybody else woulda sung that k-k-kountry and hurt poor, dead Hank Williams' drunken feelings, but you made it sound so pathetic and lonely. Subtext: "I was born to expect less." Moldy honey.

And Hank Williams, no longer drunk, just dead. Or maybe they let you stay drunk in heaven, I dunno, probly. I mean that'd be the decent thing to do, make you a drunken angel, but clean from heaven's ablutions. Hank leered his saddest leer down on you from somewhere in the ether. Crooning now: "*Come check me out of my loneliest hell.*"

God, Vic, stop singing.

And I actually—girl that I am, girl I never intended to be—welled up because we were, all four of us, so systemically sad. Why? We laughed harder than anybody. We were so ni-i-i-i-i-ice, we read like a personals ad (Billy: "a personal sad"). We loved snow and saltwater and children and old movies. We loved strange and vanilla and playing our own particular game from the right angle. We were *healthy*, of all things, so as not to upset the balance of Buddha nature and gunplay. *Enough with the sad, I'm sick of it.*

"No! I meant that," I insisted. "No sad music, James Victor. Let me be happy for a minute."

"Okay, Martha Kristin. Go."

"Go . . . happy?" I glanced over at Tina and Billy leaning on the desk, waiting for room keys, tried to flick your heartbreaking melody outta my head.

"Spell it out." This was a challenge. "Tell me the happy and I'll adopt it, but you must be convincing and you gotta convince *me*."

"That's impossible."

"No, it ain't. I promise, I'll try."

I studied your inscrutable expression, posture and vibe to see if you were fuckin' with me, but I couldn't tell. *Okay . . . motels. Cheap ones.* "I like that we belong here," I started. "Honestly, here. And we're nowhere. To us, anyway, nowhere we know." You nodded warmly. "That cheap motels are all essentially the same, so it feels like a home. Ish."

Blank stare. "We don't belong."

"Okay." I thought for a second. "But we aren't expected to, so take that off the table."

"You got it."

"Dry as the desert, but they still somehow smell like mold. And always up. I mean, awake. In perpetual motion, so they defy the laws of physics *and* thermodynamics."

You continued to stare blankly. "Kinda bullshit."

"Yeah. I just mean that they feel like stepping up into a dream."

"Okay, now *that's* the gayest thing you ever said."

I sighed. "It's the *ish* that's important: home-ish. Cuz any other home is gonna be a delineation and therefore potentially alienating."

Blanker stare. "Right."

"I like . . . buckets of ice," I continued. "We always gotta fill our buckets with ice. What's all that ice for?"

Even blanker stare.

"But I like it. Safe, clean ice. People retire to Florida to get *away* from ice but motels celebrate it."

"Reach."

"Okay, but I still meant it."

"*Florida . . .* ," you sang. This was one of your most beautiful songs.

"Where are our room keys?" I interrupted. Billy and Tina were now slumped over the desk while the clerk typed and typed . . . and typed. I picked up one of those little coffee creamers; the awful, flavored kind. There was a whole bowl of 'em sitting on the plastic table, no coffee in sight. "I like that we've been living on these things for weeks now." I read the top. "Irish Cream." Think about it, all we ever eat is motel coffee with this shit in it. Can't have any nutritional value. Barely any calories . . . proves that we live on music."

Beat. "No."

I rolled my eyes. You were impossible. Noticed that Billy was trying to explain to the desk clerk that you and Tina wanted the handicapped room, not us; asked if it was okay to switch keys. The desk clerk wasn't following.

"Okay," I fell back onto the vinyl love seat and began a dreamy litany I knew you would ignore. Just talking to myself over the infomercial that murmured and flashed above us on an almost widescreen TV. "I like sucking in chlorinated air over shallow green swimming pools with patches of snow outside between us and highways, the highways between us and farms. I like the minimum-wage cleaning staff who're sweet to us and to each other. Who get up at four a.m. and bust their asses to pay for their double-wides and drink Diet Coke for breakfast and hang outside the back of the motel in the freezing cold to smoke cigarettes and talk to each other while they wait for lazy salesmen to get out of bed so they can clean their rooms and go back home to their kids. I like that they watch Jerry Springer while they clear the styrofoam breakfast plates of families who have a little bit over them, like they aren't broken; the dad didn't take off one night like the dad in their family did, or they got a little bit more money maybe or just some kinda wherewithal that saw 'em through high school. And they care about Jerry Springer's guests' problems and discuss 'em over their breakfast cigarettes in the parking lot and I like how their hair is wrecked from bleach and permanents and you can't tell how old they are, probly *much* younger than they look, but the bleach and the permanents are still for making 'em look pretty. They aren't gonna give up because they haven't *yet*. And I like that their teeth are stained from coffee and cigarettes and broken from Coke and bad boyfriends, but they smile anyway and they always say good morning to us and they become grandmothers in their thirties and they love those grandbabies and—"

"Gotcha." Your face was deadly serious.

I looked up, amazed that you were still there.

Hank Williams bequeathed your heartbreaking song to the subculture of motel maids in a drunken angel stupor. "I get it," you muttered. "Salt o' the earth."

"*Sweet* o' the earth," I corrected.

"A home . . . ish." You nodded. "Eat candy. Gotcha. I'm a dickhead."

"No. But everybody *is* better than us."

"Yeah." You looked angry and sad. "I know." Tina appeared with the handi-room key and your falling-apart suitcase and suddenly, you were gone, wheeling away. You were the only one of us who glided; it was cool. Calling over your shoulder, you old-lady-sang over your shoulder, "*You win!*"

"What?" Billy stood smiling over me with our non-handi key and *our* falling-apart suitcase. "You *never* win."

I was as shocked as he was. "I know!" Grabbing his free hand as we walked down the dry-as-a-desert, carpeted hallway, smelling of mold, I decided to feel home, safe and dry. Just for tonight. I knew there was an invisible hammer in the suitcase and I knew Billy wasn't real careful with it. But right now, Hank Williams, so lonely he could cry, was singing us down the airless corridor to our new home. Ish. Just for tonight.

Note to self: care more plus fear more equals love more. And it's so light there.

I smiled up at Billy. "Let's get *ice*!"

The next morning, while Billy and Tina were checking out and trying to explain the key switching/handi-room dealie to a clerk with part of his skull missing, you flew backwards across the parking lot in the cold sunshine, your arms flapping gently like a seagull in an updraft. The sleeves of your lumberjacky flannel shirt flapped as you rolled gently to a stop next to a jeep. Opening the door of the jeep, you grabbed a pack of cigarettes off the passenger seat. "Got a match?"

"Nope." I was trying to coax a junkyard dog out of the empty lot next door and into my arms, using a stale donut as bait.

"That dog is so goddamn ugly!" you shouted.

"So am I!" I shouted back.

"You're not ugly, just deformed!"

"Right! Thank you!"

"Hey, so's he! He's only got three legs!"

Oh yeah. I hadn't noticed. "And I only got two!" Tearing off a piece of stiff, glazed dough, I held it out as far away from my body as I could. "C'mon, buddy. It's donuts ... you like donuts." The muddy, tilted mongrel studied me suspiciously. "Pretty sure he likes donuts, too! We have so much in common!"

"How do you know he likes donuts?" you yelled, slamming the door of the jeep.

"Everybody likes donuts!"

"*You* don't!" You shook the remaining cigarettes out of the pack and onto your lap. "Hey, matches!"

"No, I don't! That's why he can have mine!" The dog took a step toward me, then sat down. "Damn it," I muttered.

Lighting a cigarette with your fists, you wheeled back across the parking lot against the wind to watch me and the dog stare at each other. "My arm's gettin' sore," I said, still holding the donut in the air. "C'mon, dog-dude . . . you're hungry and I'm lonely."

"A match made in deformed heaven." You smoked and watched. Nobody moved. Billy ran out of the hotel into the parking lot. I watched him open the door to the van and get in, then I turned back to the dog. "It won't come any closer until you guess its name."

"Elliot?" I asked the dog. It blinked. "Bob? Tom? Wally?"

"Dumbass. Those aren't dog names."

I looked at you. "What was your rabbit named?"

"Vic."

I tried taking a step toward the dog and it yawned warily. "That's not a rabbit name."

Smoking at me, you put yourself in storytelling mode, elbows poking out. "He was a bitch. A fun-ass bitch."

"Was he a dickhead?"

"Yep."

"Then Vic *was* a good name for him." Over your shoulder, I saw Billy sitting in the driver's seat, staring. A long, deep, green-eyed stare, hypnotizing and strange. Startled, I tilted my head at him, trying to see through his gaze, but it wasn't to me, or for me, it was *through* me. Something between a sharp wind and a cool breeze; bet he didn't even know he was doing it. Then suddenly, he jumped outta the van and ran back into the hotel.

I stared after him, then took another step toward the dog. It turned its head to the side, ready to run. "I think he wants to come on tour with us."

"Billy ain't never gonna let that thing in your van. Little Vic loved pizza." You actually giggled. That weird, woody, old-lady giggle that only memories could bring on. "If you tried to keep a pizza secret from him? Or if you just didn't share? He'd thump."

"A pizza secret?" I took another step toward the dog and it leaned on its missing leg somehow. "He'd thump?"

"You never saw a rabbit thump?"

"I don't know, maybe I have. What's thumping?" I tossed a piece of donut to the dog, who snatched it up, swallowed it without chewing. "There you go, Steve. I knew you liked donuts."

Dropping your cigarette on the ground, you ran over it with your chair studiously. "*Steve?*"

"He looks like the Six Million Dollar Man. Steve Austin."

"No, he doesn't." You looked up. "Oh wow, he does."

"What's thumping?"

Fishing around under your crotch, you found another cigarette and the book of matches. "I always lose shit in these bojangle trousers."

I glanced at your pants, then turned back to watch Steve Austin watch me. "You *do* wear tap-dancin' pants. How come?"

"Skinny legs."

I threw the rest of the donut to Steve, who ate it and walked away, toward an overflowing dumpster. "'Bye, Steve! I love you!" I sat down on the curb in front of you. "What's thumping?"

"A mad rabbit'll—"

I laughed. "A *mad rabbit*?"

"Shut up and listen." You began to light another cigarette with your fists; a long, difficult process.

I stared after Steve Austin. "How'd he know I was out of donuts?"

"*Shut. Up.*" The wind that blew you backwards like a seagull was now putting matches out. "Fuck."

I watched Steve nose around the dumpster that he preferred to my loving arms and pastry. "How *did* he know I was out of donuts?"

"You stopped smelling like 'em."

"Oh." When you got your second cigarette lit, you sucked half of it down to keep it lit in the wind. "I should try to smell more like donuts."

"Yep." You eyed me through the smoke blowing around your ears and over your shoulders.

"Say it," I urged. "I'm bored. Say the thumping thing."

"An angry rabbit'll—"

"What was Steve Austin's real name?" I interrupted. "I mean, who played him."

"Lee Majors." We watched Lee's dog butt walk away. "The six million dollar junkyard dog."

"G'bye Lee!" I called. "Don't forget me!"

"He's already forgotten you."

"With a belly full o' donut? How can that be?"

Balancing the cigarette on your right hand—your driving glove hand—you waved smoke away with your left. "Love and stomachs are different things."

"Not *that* different." I sighed. "I'm showing him I care."

You squinted into the hotel to see what was slowing down checkout. "Little Vic'd sit under the table or under wherever you put your pizza. And you'd hear *bang, bang, bang*, but like banging made out of cotton."

"A banging made out of cotton? Little rabbit feet?"

"*Big* rabbit feet. Little Vic was a big rabbit and he used his biggest feet to thump. The hind ones." Your cigarette had blown down to the filter, but you kept smoking it. "He did *not* have skinny legs."

I stood up. Now I knew what thumping was and Lee Majors was gone. Figured the rest of your story was gonna just be rambling embellishment. "You want some shitty coffee?"

"No, I don't."

"You mean yes, you do?"

"I mean yes, I do."

Pulling open the front door of the motel, I called over my shoulder, "Wish I knew rabbit Vic," and you nodded.

"Yes," you called back, still staring after Lee Majors' butt. "Yes, you do."

The desk clerk's skull was missing such a huge piece of itself that his head was shaped like . . . I dunno, Pac-man. I'm not sure Billy and Tina were ever able to adequately explain the fact that we'd switched rooms, but not cuz this guy's damaged skull had damaged his brain; he seemed to be hard of hearing. Every sentence I heard him utter began with, "What?"

Maybe it was just a nervous tic or something. Now all three of them were laughing. Billy had made a friend, as usual. He's always had a thing for people with misshapen heads. Also, deaf people. So this was, like, a match made in deformed heaven. Just like me and Steve Austin. I mean Lee Majors.

I raised my eyebrows at him to ask if we should maybe . . . *drive away from here*, but his grin was for Pac-man head, not me. Or, at least, it was *about* Pac-man head. "Want some coffee?" I asked him sweetly. "For the *drive*?"

He didn't seem to hear, said something about football to Pac-man head, then grabbed the motel receipt and told the guy to take care of himself. Tina already had her back to them, her motel receipt sticking out of the back pocket of her jeans.

"Want some coffee?" I asked her, holding out a styrofoam cup and fishing around in the bowl of creamers for the grossest kind. "Maple Walnut!" I cried happily, holding it up. Slowly, she shook her head and left. Billy eyed me carefully and mouthed, "*Don't do it.*"

"Don't do *what*?" I asked loudly.

He pressed his lips together, grim, and crossed the room. "*Don't drink the coffee,*" he hissed under his breath. "*I'll explain later.*"

"Geez, okay."

He never did explain why this terrible coffee was more terrible than the terrible coffee we drank *every* morning. I imagined it had something to do with Pac-man head's missing skull quadrant. Maybe it fell off that morning while he was brewing the lobby coffee and it was still floating in the pot, bouncing off the bottom of the carafe and rising to the warm, oily surface.

Or Lee Majors' missing leg. That coulda found its way into the thick, black liquid and turned it all bloody and furry, you never know. Or some wholly other unholy event that befell the stained Mr. Coffee, twenty-four-cup-size coffee maker and the Folgers medium-roast filter pack within.

It was an eight-hour drive to the next club. I had lots of time to think.

Austin, Texas. Tina and I stood in a dizzying empty lot, soaking up the morning dew, the flittering moths, fluttering sugarberry leaves. I turned to her, almost for help. "Texas and Scotland," I said, gutted by the air. "Crazy. The land can move me to tears."

"I get that," Tina nodded. "But I never feel like I belong."

"Mm-hm . . . I get *that*."

"I only belong in one place."

Stunned, I tore my eyes from the silver sage lot and studied her. "You belong somewhere?"

"Sure," she shrugged. "Home."

Tina has a home.

Which was—obviously—the difference between Tina and *us*.

Woke up one morning and stayed in bed long enough to watch Billy sleep for a few minutes. I tried to remember where we were. Couldn't. No idea where we were, didn't really care. A safe motel room is a catacomb; you don't have to care where you are, you barely exist.

Billy's invisible hammer lay quiet on his bedside table cuz when he slept, he *was* careful. He was intricate, elaborately peaceful, complete. Sometimes when he woke up, he'd still be this way for a little while. This was a holy time. A green ocean in his green eyes, steady. Then he'd shake off that peace, grab his hammer, and get back to the erratic heart murmur he wore around, running up and down peaks and valleys like he was following his own EKG. Holey, fighting off predators.

I turned away. Faces that move you hurt when life has not always been gentle. And nutty dreams had left an odd jumble of hope and hopelessness, home and homelessness, the tendrils of which were stepping aside to allow another day to begin. Billy was hope, home, and a shaky heartbeat.

I have a song called "Hope" and a song called "Home." Neither of which have ever offered me explanations or medicine. And I couldn't shake off in-between. Wondered if that's what prayer was: going to in-between on purpose and sitting there. It was peaceful, but painful, too. The hope part, the last tendril. That one hurt somehow. Then even hope faded.

So quietly, I reached out to pull the thick motel curtain aside and see the day that was gonna take over for those smoky dreams. Tugged a little too hard, I guess, cuz the window shade beneath sproinged up into itself with a *whoosh* and crashed to the floor. I looked at Billy, alarmed, as he opened one eye in the splashing sunshine. "What'd you do *now*?" he asked, not unkindly, and shut his eye again, turned over.

Stupid sunshine. It *is* poisonous. Blasted Billy's peace away in a spill I couldn't clean up. I was the sunshine pussy, you were right. Scareder of poison sunshine than . . . *sacreder, scareder, scared o' sacred sun.*

Remembered where we were. *LA.* On the nightstand was a blue can of mineral water I'd brought from the dressing room last night. I sat up and opened it. This was the loudest beverage can opening that ever happened: a rifle shot of a *pop*, then the can hissed like a flat tire. Hissed for like, ever. I winced, studying Billy's back and waiting for the noise to stop.

Billy put his pillow over his head. "Shhhh . . ." I hoped he didn't think I was drinking a beer in bed first thing in the morning. Hog children are okay, but as a grown woman, I had more trailer park in me than he was real comfortable with.

Never been in this hotel room before but it was every hotel room I'd ever been in. The TV, the staticky carpet, the hollow bathroom door. I looked around, comfortable on earth's plane for a minute. "Hope" was stuck in my head. You hated hope, said it was misguided. And when you sang "Free of Hope," I always felt for you that you couldn't hold a seed of growth and a seed of disappointment at the same time; you know, *ride* that human train. Billy sided with you and called hope doubt, but remained patient with my plan for magic. He knew I had to chant *it's gonna be okay* or I wouldn't be okay, whether "it" was or not. Tina fell somewhere in the middle. So mathematically, I guess you won the hope debate, though I haven't stopped hoping.

The blue can shook in my hand. *Earthquake*, I thought. But nothing else was shaking, just the can. So I listened harder to my memory of you singing about shaking off ghosts and albatrosses like the past and hope, watched Billy's shoulder breathe. He once told me he dreamt about the Blue Plate Special at the Chinese restaurant on our island, how the lunch menu was a good deal, cuz it came with an eggroll. *That is one self-actualized dude*, I'd thought to myself. But really, a Chinese menu could cover up a hole *and* a hammer, so who knows?

If this was LA, you and Tina weren't down the hall like you usually were, you were staying in a . . . yurt? Maybe I made that up or dreamt it. Wherever you were, though, you were sleeping. You guys slept; we didn't, really. Billy *would* have slept if he wasn't shackled to jumpy me, probly. I knew your little bags of Chesnutt food—trail mixes and dried goofiness—were open and placed strategically around your room, like you were expecting goats or hippies. Suddenly, I wished we could just freeze in this alternate reality of lost . . . become *easy* people. I wished it so hard that I wondered if this aching with hope was prayer. *Or maybe prayer's the in-between thing, I dunno.*

We will never be free: a little comforting, a little terrifying. At least we reach for each other. The can shook in my hand, so I placed it carefully on the bedside table. "Shhhh . . ." Billy chuckled.

That night someone requested a song Tina didn't like cuz it was about another woman, someone who'd come before her. I raised my eyebrows and shook my head at the guy; didn't wanna hear you scolded ever again. Didn't want you to do shit but hold onto that woman. You played the song, anyway, though. Songs happen, I guess.

"If you don't mind," I said into the mic tersely while the audience was still clapping for you, "for the rest of the evening, please only request songs that are about his *wife*." I couldn't help it. Stupid. Like they'd know which songs were about Tina. I just felt like you needed help not fucking up. None of my business, probly. You were just such a lucky dickhead.

After the show, we were sitting in front of the stage, waiting to leave and watching drunk stragglers wander around the room. "The Aimless," you called those with poor aim and nowhere to go, who couldn't understand the bouncers' call: "You don't have to go home, but you can't stay here." I always felt like I understood that call deep in my bones. They didn't need to yell it at me, it was a given. I lived my life by the bouncer call.

A man wearing an "X" T-shirt approached us, grinning shyly. "Thank you!" he said. "You helped me win a bet tonight." We said nothing, waited for him to explain. "My friends didn't believe that Kristin Hersh and Vic Chesnutt were married."

I glanced at you. "You mean to each other?" I asked him. "Ew."

You, smirking at me: "Naw, we ain't married. She's married to a *real* man. That yelling guy over there." You pointed across the room to where Billy was, indeed, yelling; that hammer came in handy sometimes.

"My husband is from New York," I explained. "And somebody's gotta yell," I told you. "Ain't gonna be any of us hog children."

"Nope," you agreed. "It takes a real man."

Me, to the smiling guy who'd stopped smiling: "And Vic's married to a real woman. That one over there," I said, pointing to Tina, who stood by Billy's side, his silent partner in yelling.

"*Beautiful Tina, wake unto me . . . ,*" you sang.

We watched Billy finish his rant, Tina folding her arms in agreement. "We wouldn't get *paid* half the time if he didn't yell," I pointed out.

"I know it," you nodded.

The guy who'd made the bet looked crestfallen. "Are you sure you two aren't married?" he asked, looking from one of us to the other.

What the hell kinda question is that? We just stared at him. "Ew," I repeated.

"Broken people," you said offhandedly, "marry *real* people. So they can fix us." The guy looked baffled.

"We need . . . help," I explained. "How could you make that bet?" I asked him. "We were just talking about Tina in the set."

You looked disgusted. "How *much* did you bet?"

"Fifty bucks. Bought a round of drinks."

Shaking your head at him: "You lost."

I'm trying to remember now how it felt to be so absolutely certain that Billy and Tina were gonna fix us. It must have been wonderful.

So you guys actually were staying in a kind of yurt in Joshua Tree some friend-fan had given you for the night. Billy and I drove in from LA to see y'all and smell sage. We both noticed immediately that Tina blended somehow. Pulling into the driveway, we saw her squint-talking over the chain-link fence to tweaker neighbors who stood in the sun with their morning beers and muddy dogs, hosing down their dirt. Funny . . . she was the only one of us with a home, but she blended. Inside the slanted dwelling, you seemed just as at home in the shadowed little rooms, Mexican blankets covering the walls.

You told us there'd been a sing-a-long the night before, and a drum circle. Tina said no, that never happened. You said yeah it did, she only denied it cuz she'd been singing one of *your* songs, Kristin, and now she's embarrassed. Tina asked if we wanted some coffee or maybe a beer. Added that no, that couldn't have happened cuz she can't sing. Well, you did anyway, you told her and Billy and I sat on a red and gold carpet, happily making plans to come back. To come back and breathe in more sage.

Billy, coming to a decision: "Let's meet in the desert."

Tina: "We just did."

Billy: "No, for real, to stay. Find places to live, be desert people."

You: "I wanna be desert people."

Howdy !

Here is a box
of candy for
you to enjoy.
I want to see
ya'll soon and

then live in your
desert outhouse
Love
Vic

Card from Vic.

Me: "Yeah, okay. Let's do it. Sunshine and sage. Busted fences make busted neighbors."

You: "You hate sunshine."

Me: "So do you. But you can't hate sunshine in the desert; it's a given. Like immersion therapy."

Billy: "True. It's cleansing here. Strips you clean."

You: "We can be bones."

Me: "We can be shriveled-apple-shrunken-head-doll people."

Billy: "Wide open space'll give us wide open time."

Tina, wide-eyed and sober: "We will meet you here in one year."

The next year, Billy and I settled into a house on forty acres of pristine high desert land. We learned coyotes and roadrunners (both carnivorous), then Joshua trees, vultures, gun-toting, dune-buggy-building, shavedy-headed neighbors, rattlesnakes, and the phases of the moon. These constancies made the busy-ness of humanity seem ephemeral. Daily news, disappearing then repeating itself, people rushing around, checking their numbers: bank accounts and ages, scales and gas gauges. They looked at their watches instead of at the sky. A small, small picture. We learned big picture in the desert. Wide open space bought us wide open time, Billy'd guessed right. The moon is a *big* picture; it's the fucking *moon*, after all.

Y'all never showed up.

A morning in San Francisco: you rolling backwards down an almost vertical hill. "Pancakes come faster when you fall to them!"

Tina first covered her mouth with her hands, then covered her eyes. Billy jumped out and reached for your chair, but you were gone, streaking past people walking dogs, carrying groceries, and holding toddlers' hands. "*Wheeeeeeeeee!*"

We watched, frozen on the sidewalk as, pedestrians jumping out of your way, cars honking, you sped backwards through a crosswalk against the light. Gliding up onto the curb, you whizzed past the doorway of a diner, then screeched to a halt and rolled back up to it. "Pancakes!" you announced, peering into the window with interest.

Spinning around to face us from the opposite side of the street, you stared, blank. The three of us stared back, unable to breathe, as you held out your hands in frustration. "Come *on*!"

Somehow, we talked you into staying at a nice hotel in Seattle, though you balked spectacularly. "Nice is shitty! You'll see. Don't got your beloved toothless maids in no *nice* hotel, just white people gonna treat us like shit."

"White people?" Your reverse snobbery could be really annoying sometimes. Like when I just wanted to sleep in a bed without *fleas*. Without the trashy couple next door fucking or screaming at each other. Wanted a breakfast other than Folgers Crystals and Irish Creamer. "Why would they treat us like shit?"

"Cuz we *are* shit. Duh-uh. And they know it."

"But we get a deal at this place! It'll be cheaper than Motel 6."

"I know. You said that," you griped. But you weren't gonna make me sleep next door to white trash couples *or* get flea-bitten, you just liked griping. Of course, you made me pay for my win. When Billy and I got to our room, the phone was already ringing. Billy picked it up.

"Hello?" He listened expressionlessly, then handed the phone to me. "*You* talk to him."

Aw, geez. I cringed and took a deep breath, then sighed it out. "Yeah?"

"Bedspread jizz."

"Huh?"

"Last handi-room guest jerked off before he checked out, left me and my wife a nice little blob o' jizz on the bedspread. Scratch little."

"Oh wow. Are you sure that's what it is?"

A loud squawk. "You think I don't know jizz when I see it?!"

I held the phone away from my ear. "Sorry."

"I blame you."

"I know you do, but hold on. At Motel 6, they'd just be like, *so what? we put jizz in all the rooms*, but here they gotta keep up appearances. Complain to the front desk. They'll chew out housekeeping, but they might comp you your room or give you the presidential suite or something."

"The president handi?" you grumbled. "I forgit." And hung up.

Suddenly, I had a thought, and turned to my grinning husband. "Billy, what room are they in?"

"One eleven."

Dialing you back, I hoped you weren't already yelling at some poor desk clerk. You picked up the phone but didn't say anything. "Vic?"

"Whadda *you* want?"

"Don't say 'jizz.' Say . . . say . . ." I squinted at Billy for help. He shook his head sadly. "You are the hog children."

"Well, I know," I said, frustrated. "Help us."

"Ejaculate."

You heard him. "Gotcha."

I smiled, impressed. "Ejaculate." I repeated into the phone. "Classy. And be nice. You'll get more."

"Oh, I'll be a prince. No dickhead, Vic Chesnutt." I heard a *click* as you tried to hang up. "Hello?" you demanded.

"Hi."

" *Kristin*?? Will you get off the *phone*? I wanna give white people shit!"

So all you got was a clean bedspread and a gift box of nuts—"jizz nuts" we called 'em for the rest of the tour, which ensured that they just sat on the backseat, untouched. But at least you got to squawk at white people, right?

Vancouver: your arms were flapping around again. I'd tried to spin the fluorescent-lit dressing room with hippie chick candles, but you wouldn't let me turn off the lights, so my candles were pretty impotent. "You're making my candles impotent," I grumbled.

"They aren't *impotent*," you squawked, "they're lame."

Billy sighed. "She likes it dark. She's not gonna be nice until it's dark and her candles are potent again."

Your arms were flapping. Slowly, but definitely flapping. Cuz you were somewhere else entirely; you weren't listening, didn't care about mood lighting. Those chicken bone arms'd just start flapping of their own accord when you had a story to tell. "I had this gun . . ."

For an angel, you weren't very angelic.

The dressing room door opened and a tattooed waif entered, struggling with a plastic bin full of ice and beer. Tina and Billy stood up to help him, but not before the kid's weak arms let a few hundred ice cubes slide out of the bin and onto the floor. "Sorry," he wheezed, his thin, pasty biceps straining. Covered in red bumps, they stuck out of a black T-shirt with a white face on it.

Billy took the bin from him and placed it on the counter. "No problem," he told the kid, slapping him on the back. This almost knocked the waif boy over and he coughed, glancing at you out of the corner of his eye.

"I know you," you snarled at him. The waif said nothing, didn't move.

"Aw, shit," Tina muttered under her breath.

"Whose face is that?" you demanded. The kid looked baffled. "Whose face is on your shirt?"

"Oh." He pulled the T-shirt away from his slender rib cage and studied the face upside down. "Wittgenstein."

"Oh yeah?" you smirked, done with him, so he left. Tina sighed. Billy opened a beer and handed it to me, then opened one for Tina and one for himself. You didn't get any cuz you weren't allowed.

"I had this gun," you repeated, still mad at the waif kid, for some reason. "And—"

I took a sip of my beer. "Why?"

"Why what?"

Tina nudged me with her elbow. "When you ask questions, the stories get longer."

"Sorry." I gazed at you with rapt attention. "Go on."

You, annoyed: "I had a gun because every kid in Georgia has a gun. Didn't you? You had a hog."

"It wasn't actually *my* hog . . ." I muttered, embarrassed. "I didn't *own* it."

Tina tipped her head to the side and a few little braids fell over her shoulder. "I think girls have fewer guns."

"Oh." This seemed to bore you. "What did you do if you couldn't shoot nuthin'?" you growled, amazed. "Like . . . arts and crafts or some-fuckin'-thing? Pot-fuckin'-holders?" But you didn't wait for a response; even your own questions bored you when you were snarly. Funny thing was, snarly made you happy, so you read as: sweet. This woulda killed you to know. Bitch Chesnutt, the sweetheart. But we liked you in this mood, it was entertaining. "I was supposed to shoot animals with it, practice on little ones and build up to big ones. Squirrel to deer, you know—"

"Well, that doesn't make sense," I said.

You sighing, frustrated: "*What?*"

"Isn't a smaller target harder to hit? And squirrels are fast."

"Yeah . . . and wily," added Billy.

"Deer just freeze, right?" I pointed my beer bottle at you. "You shoulda gone deer to *squirrel*."

Billy nodded. "That's what we do in New York."

Tina nudged me again. "You're making the story longer."

Ignoring her, I demanded, "And what about the traps you're always talking about? You trapped animals *and* shot them?"

"Did you trap them first and then shoot them?" Billy asked, looking askance. "That's not very sporting."

You, glaring at the three of us: "In this story—"

I turned to Tina. "You have, like, twice as many braids as you had yesterday. Everything okay?" She shrugged and fingered a few braids, looking thoughtful.

"In this story," you repeated angrily, "I don't shoot any animals."

Billy drained his beer and dropped the bottle back into the ice. "Good." He glanced at me. "Opening act's done. God-awful, did you see him?"

"I did. Crummy, crummy, crummy. Not cool. That was a mean thing to do into a microphone."

"I almost felt sorry for him," said Billy, checking his watch. "Almost." He looked down at your wife. "Let's go set up." Tina stood, still counting her braids with her fingers as Billy held the door open for her. We could hear music playing over the PA until the door swung shut. Flush/lurch. Then it was quiet and we were alone.

I bet Billy wishes I were a good woman, like Tina, I thought miserably. *My ugly is so goddamn ugly. And my evil is so goddamn evil. Stupid music. Not enough sweetness in the world to cover anything as bitter as music. No Jolly Rancher or tonic water's gonna save my goddamned soul. This is why I can't fill his holes.*

I noticed you staring at me and snapped out of it, remembered your story. You hated inner monologues, especially pathetic ones. Said you could smell 'em with a ten-foot pole and it was true, you could. Suddenly, you were no longer sweet or entertaining. Self-conscious, I drank my beer and waited patiently for you to finish your story. I'm a polite southern girl, after all. A hog child. I *try* to cover the bitter with sweetness.

For some reason, you were doing that shattering blue portal thing with your eyes; the pinpoint of black hole judgment. I whipped my head around to see if there was somebody behind me you were trying to kill, but no. It was me. "So . . . what did you shoot?" I asked, uncomfortable. You looked away, said nothing. Which was even worse than trying to kill me with your eyes. "Was it a person?" I was so ready for you to say you'd killed somebody. In fact, I'd already decided that you had. Who was it, though? Like, the mailman? A neighbor? Your teacher? Another kid?

"Nuthin."

I watched you look at the wall and try to kill *it*. "You shot nothing? That's not a very good story."

Those vivid blue lasers left the wall and bore into my eye sockets. "I shot a tree until it fell down."

I can't tell you how sad that made me. I forgot my Billy stomachache and saw before me this whole movie of your childhood, as vivid as your blue portals. James Victor Chesnutt, one *s*, two *t*'s. Little, fat southern kid, dressed in fatigues and a grimy T-shirt. Eats candy outta the candy dish on the coffee table, goes to Sunday school, is a closet atheist. His parents tell him he was adopted, so he decides he's different, doesn't belong. Never forgets this for a single moment. Watches *Speed Racer* before anybody else is up on Saturday mornings. Wants a pet chimp. Traps possums. Is scared of rabbits. Dances in a school play, gets beat up, never dances again. His only friends are mentally retarded. He beats *them* up which gets him beat up by other kids again. Repeat: never dances again.

I knew all this, but adding *shoots trees 'til they fall down* was like making me watch your home movies until I broke down and cried. That kid was gonna drive drunk one night when he was eighteen and . . . well, now he wants to be a ghost. A *ghewst*.

"I'm sorry." It was all I could think of to say.

When the waif walked back in and told us we had to go on in five minutes, he stood slightly behind you, to your right, kneeling down the way people do so they don't tower above you. Unfortunately, this posture is reminiscent of that of a person speaking to a child and it bugs you. I knew this because you made a very Vic face when people did it. You made the same face when other men had to lift your chair onto a stage or up a flight of stairs. It was an awful face. I don't want to describe it cuz I don't like thinking about it, but what it meant was: don't you fucking look at me.

So I guess there was shame in you after all. I mean, you were pretty good at convincing the rest of us that we *shared* an agony and that's what shame is good for. Take a song like

"Myrtle." You could turn a room full of healthy people out for a good time into sick children dragged by donkeys through the underbrush and still claim that it was a lush, verdant life we were living. Were we ashamed? I don't know. Too many of us feeling humiliation to be humiliated, really. And your spin was always lovely. We don't belong, but we don't belong *together*. Best we can do. Snarly-sweet.

Anyway, the waif was positioned in such a way that you could use the alternate arm motion you learned in physical therapy after your car accident to lift your driving-glove fist into the air, elbow first, and backhand him in the face. Which you did. Quickly and powerfully.

The kid's knees buckled as he stumbled backwards, holding his jaw, and leaned against the wall, slipping down a few inches. I imagine my eyes were huge, but all I remember is sitting there holding my beer, thinking, *the only thing he killed was a tree?*

"I said I was sorry," mumbled the waif, still holding his jaw. He looked at both of us, then left, club music filling the room briefly as the door shut behind him.

Blank stare.

"What did he *do*?" I asked quietly.

You rubbed your driving-glove hand with the other one. "Nuthin."

We were playing our sets together then, both of us on stage, trading songs back and forth and talking. Talking music, talking shit, telling stories. We laughed real hard; you, me, the listeners. But we welled up, too, of all things . . . and that was pretty out of character for you and me, both. I'd heard of the laughing/crying thing, just like I'd heard of the love/hate thing, but I could never do that math until songs' unbalanced dichotomy kicked down my door. Sometimes music is just a little bit too much is all. And I loved and hated it for making me laugh and cry.

That car accident left you with exactly—and *only*—what you needed. What you needed to do this, to play songs that were just a little bit too much. Oddly, a car accident was what made *me* play music, too. Not a lifetime in a wheelchair, but as you used to say: "time spent on your ass is time invested." My accident made me hear songs, yours made you play them.

One night on this tour, you called me an *ocean witch*; something about salt and viscera. "Well, you're a mountain shaman," I told you back and thought, *broken in all the right places*.

You nodded, your eyes full of hate. "But I would give anything to play guitar like you, Kristin."

That was the meanest thing you ever said to me. I wanted to grab my jaw and stumble backwards into the wall, like the waif boy did when you slugged *him*. And what did I do to deserve it?

Nuthin'.

Arching, contorting, twisting, your torso rose up, your grandfather's little nylon-strung acoustic banging against the arm of your wheelchair, your Bojangle trousers slipping down around your hips as your legs crossed and uncrossed themselves. This was thinking for you. Most of us think with our brains, you did it with your whole body.

"The swan songs!" you decided and the audience clapped, for some reason. There was no way they could've known what you were talking about. My swan song was "Hungry" and yours was "Second Floor," both unreleased. Neither one a "swan song" per se, they just both mentioned swans, which we thought was kinda funny.

"Nah . . ." scrunching my nose up at you, "I mean, okay, but I don't wanna." I addressed the crowd. "Don't clap, you don't know what he's talking about."

"Well, *I* know what I'm talking about," you whined. "We each have a song with a swan in it, which I think is a pretty cool coincidence."

Tuning my guitar, I muttered, "It's just a regular coincidence. A cool one'd be if they were also *thematically related*. Or even in the same key or something, but they just got swans in 'em. And just for a second."

You seated yourself again and fixed your pants so that they weren't falling down. "It ain't my fault yours sucks."

I thought about this. "It is . . . sort of. Blowing me off the stage makes it look like I suck more than I actually do."

"True." You nodded. "Sorry about that. You will never be famous because of your suckage."

"Famous *is* suckage. You don't get famous without sucking."

You wanted desperately to believe this snottiness that came so easily to me. A flash of pain, a familiar look in your eye. You, a genius, would die thinking you were a failure. Addressing the audience: "Y'all ever stay in a motel that ain't as cheap as the ones we stay in?"

DON'T SUCK, DON'T DIE

"We stay in the crummiest ones," I offered helpfully.

"And they got . . ." You held your hands up over your guitar, making them into a circle. "They got those fucked up, little circular mirrors?"

I tried to look as dumbfounded as I am every time I see those weird little mirrors. "Right next to the mirror!"

"Yeah." Three whole syllables you drew out of the word "yeah." You dropped your hands and they thudded onto the guitar, playing an open E minor seventh that rang under your ringing voice. "And you go, *okay, lemme have a look . . . after all, it's just a mirror, what could it do to me*?" I stopped tuning my guitar to listen. "And there's your circular face looking back at you, no biggie." You glanced at me out of the corner of your right eye. "Then you see in the mirror that the back of this mirror is another *mirror*."

"What's the point?" I agreed, nodding along, and you pointed at me pointedly. "Who needs the *one* mirror?" I asked for emphasis.

"Exactimundo, queen bitch from hell."

". . . I'm sorry?"

"Cuz-you-flip-the-circle-over-and-suddenly-you-are-face-to-face-with-the-ugliest-face-you-ever-saw-and: it's yours!"

Nodding, I said ruefully, "The pore enlarger."

"The pore enlarger," you repeated.

I waited. Nothing. "So . . . why am I . . . a what? A bitch from hell?"

"You're a bitch from hell because that mirror is you! You are the pore enlarger. Cuzza you, I know—up close and personal that I am the ugliest son of a bitch that ever was!"

This was the *nicest* thing you ever said to me. And your voice rose in volume and pitch over the course of the sentence. You hit notes I could only dream of hitting. Then you calmed down completely, dropping that insane voice at least an octave or two. "And you're a *queen*, cuz you'd have people killed if you could."

I stared at you a minute to see how serious you were. *Pretty darn.* So I looked back down at my guitar and began tuning again. "I guess that's true."

And you muttered, off mic: "You *know* that's true."

A guy in the audience yelled, "Thailand!" at you.

"Vic only takes requests," I told the guy, still tuning my guitar—I was only on the D string—"if you're prepared to offer him a fatty." And you giggled that cool, old lady giggle. "You sound like my grandmother when you laugh," I told you, killing time.

"Yep." To the crowd: "When I order a pizza? The Domino's guy always says, 'Thank you, ma'am.'"

I finished tuning the D and looked at you. "And when I order a pizza, they call me 'sir.'"

Your eyebrows rose and your jaw dropped, Little Rascals–style, for the audience's benefit. "Maybe they're just fuckin' with us."

"Maybe. You do sound like my grandma, though." My G wasn't cooperating. Hadn't changed my strings in a while and it was stretchy.

"I know it," you nodded. "And you sound like a guy." The audience laughed.

"Sorry. G-string trouble." I caught Billy's eye as he stood

side of stage, smiling at him and he smiled back. A *good* flush/lurch. The audience laughed louder. "How 'bout . . ." I rested my chin on my guitar. "You play 'pushing the paint around' and I'll listen and fiddle with my G-string."

You: "If anybody tries to shove a dollar in her G-string, she'll punch you in the face, I seen her do it." I shook my head, bewildered, having just watched you punch somebody in the face.

But instead of playing "Sad Peter Pan," you flipped me off with a dark look, which was code for *my left middle finger ain't workin' right today, so I can't play that song*. Which amazed me, because you were still playing bass, rhythm, and lead in the same songs, had been all night. "Doesn't sound right without you playing leads," was your excuse.

But I guess I could tell your distinctive fluid timing was especially fluid, especially distinctive that night. I knew that that was almost always due to you waiting for your hands to cooperate and sometimes they just didn't. I never told anybody that, though. Well, not 'til now. Because it was always so beautiful that I envied it. God is cruel but smart. He really did break you in all the right places.

"Let's play the song about ham," I offered and you looked deeply relieved.

"Right on," nodding like your head was on a pulley.

So we started "Panic Pure" and for the thousandth time, I wondered at your generosity of spirit, your willing hunger and your brain all in backwards. Wondered at the futility of you believing in fame, when the quiet stories held all dimensions effortlessly.

Interview in an Ann Arbor restaurant.

You: "*Domino's/Is all I know/About Ann Arbor's/Road show*."

Journalist: "Well, we have the university, obviously . . . fifth-largest city in Michigan . . ."

Me: "Domino's thinks I'm a man and Vic's a lady."

Journalist: "Huh."

You: "True."

Journalist: "Really? [beat] You sure you guys don't wanna order anything?"

Me: "We can order something if you *want*. I mean, if we're gonna get in trouble for just sitting here."

Journalist: "Not at all. I do a lot of interviews here, I just thought starving musicians might be . . . hungry."

You: "They got hippie food here?"

Journalist: "Tons. That's *all* they got here."

You: "Cool. Bitchin'. Cuz that's all we eat."

Me: "Plus, we eat these little . . . these little . . ."

You: "Creamers."

Journalist: "Creamers?"

Me: "Coffee creamers."

You: "Only the awful ones. Hazelnut, French Vanilla—"

Me: "Irish Cream."

You: "Our spouses do the same. We make 'em."

Journalist: "Do you mind if I record this?"

You: "Hell, no."

Journalist: "Let's talk about inspiration."

You: "No such thing."

Journalist: "Really."

Me: "He means that you could measure."

Journalist: "Interesting."

You: "A song is an orgasm."

Journalist: "Explain."

You: "I just did."

Journalist: "Explain *more*."

You: "Songs're unhappy accidents, mutations."

Journalist: "Kristin? Do you agree?"

Me: "I have no idea what a song is."

Journalist: "None whatsoever?"

Me: "Well . . . I know it's not an idea."

Journalist: "You couldn't have an idea for a song?"

Me: "You could have an idea for a *bad* song."

You: "She means brains fake you out."

Journalist: "What's a *good* song?"

Me: "Animal response."

You: "But we still don't know what a song is."

Waitress: "Can I get you guys something to drink?"

You: "*Mineral wasser mit gas.*"

Me: "He's speaking German."

Waitress: "Oh."

Journalist: "I'll just have some coffee."

Me: "Carrot juice with ginger. And wheatgrass. And bee pollen. And . . . spirulina."

You: "Stop."

Me: "Okay."

Waitress: "Carrot juice with ginger, bee pollen, spirulina, and wheatgrass. Coffee. But I didn't get the . . . German order."

Kristin: "Heinz will have a Perrier."

Vic: "That's French, dumbass." [singing] "*L'ass muet is French for dumbass.*"

Waitress: ". . . so . . . Perrier?"

You: "Perri-fuckin'-A."

Waitress: "Be back in a minute."

You: "'Bye!"

Journalist: "How is it that you don't know what a song is?"

Me: "Songs just *are*. I don't make them up."

You: "Only shitty musicians make up songs."

Me: "Yeah, that's just self-expression. Smaller than you. Whining, really."

Journalist: "Aren't your songs about you?"

You: "Well, yeah, they'd have to be, or we couldn't play 'em right."

Journalist: "And that's not self-expression . . .?"

Me: "No, no. You gotta get self-expression out of the way, *then* a song will come and tell you your stories in such a way as to make its own point. I mean, if you're a real songwriter. Not a good thing necessarily. You could just fake it instead."

Journalist: "Who is a 'real' songwriter?"

You: "They gotta be broken."

Me: "Sad but true."

Journalist: "Do you wanna be rock stars?"

You: "Yep."

Me: "Shut up. There should never have *been* rock stars cuz music is the anti-smug."

Journalist: "The anti-smug."

You: "And the anti- and the anti- and the anti- and the anti- and the anti- . . . what am I trying to say?"

Me: "What *are* you trying to say?"

You: "The anti-exhibitionist."

Me: "Oh. Yeah."

[long pause]

You: "I stutter when I think out loud."

Me: "He's from another planet."

You: "Zebulon is not another planet."

[longer pause]

Journalist: "In what state do you write your material?"

Me: "Gone."

You: "Tuned in, turned on."

Journalist: "Does it hurt?"

Me: "It hurts."

You: "It's a good hurt."

Me: "But it doesn't matter, cuz I can't feel it. My whole job is to disappear."

Journalist: "Disappear?"

You: "When you disappear, it's cuz you went to war."

Journalist: "Uh-huh. And in what state do you *perform* your material?"

You: "We are not The Singers."

Journalist: "You aren't."

You: "I *saw* him once."

Me: "I *heard* mine."

You: "Took an X-Acto knife to the drywall, trying to get to him."

Me: "Did you find him?"

You: "Nope. Never did. Fucked up the wall pretty good, though."

Walking from the restaurant to the club that night, we were accosted by a group of young men. Well, *you* were accosted; I just watched.

"Vic? Vic Chesnutt!" They crowded around you in the middle of a crosswalk. "I can't believe it's you! Are you going to the show?"

You nodded. "Yeah, they *make* me go to my shows." Cars drove around us on either side.

The boys all laughed loudly for a very long time while we waited to finish crossing the street. Their laughter faded and then picked up again while cars honked their horns and sped past us. Apparently, that was the funniest thing anybody had ever said. You were loving this. "I meant . . ." chuckled the guy, "are you on your way to the club?"

"If I don't get run over!" We crossed the street with them in a flurry of *sorry, Vic's*. Then they crowded around you on the sidewalk, leaving me out of the circle.

"If I bring some of your CDs, will you sign 'em?"

You grinned. "Bring *your* CDs, I'm keepin' mine." Now *this* was the funniest thing that anybody'd ever said, which was weird cuz it wasn't funny at all. They laughed and laughed until I was bored and wondering how to slip away while you entertained.

One of the boys, breathless: "Can I ask you a question, Vic?"

"Sure!" You looked up at him engagingly.

"Is Kristin Hersh really gonna be there?"

Screwing up your face thoughtfully, you considered this for a minute, looking genuinely confused.

". . . *who*?"

That night, you played piano instead of guitar, just because they had one at the club. You sat at a goddamn piano and played your entire set on it; played songs I'd never heard before, rolling your fists over the keys, your voice flying around the meter, crashing bass under the floating chords, melodies surfing over the top. You played, "The Wrong Piano," of all things and it was so, so . . . well, pretty.

Just a ball of everything that was you in that moment: heartbreaking goofiness. I guess heartbreaking goofiness was you *all* the time, but this was more. You said things that killed us; terrible, gorgeous things. You sang "I'm Through," which was just cruel. No barrier between your brain and your tongue, ever. Those boys had turned you on, I guess. Blew your ego bubble up enough to turn you on to your*self*.

You winked at me! And you were not a winker, but it was a winky moment and you captured it, which is just so . . . friendly. I try not to forget that wink because it was the opposite of so many looks you gave me over the years: drawn-and-quartered looks, tarred-and-feathered looks, beastly brains pouring out of your eye sockets. But I dunno, you were full of yourself, sitting at that piano in Ann Arbor, overflowing. So you winked at the only girl around: me. Barely a girl at all, just a road hog—hog child who crashed on your floor sometimes cuz my man and me always needed a safe house, a place to hide, and nobody but you and Tina would take us in and take care of us. But that wink meant *it's all a joke, so fuck it*.

Of course, you were not The Singer. You deserve no credit or blame for what happened whenever you found yourself tuned in and turned on. But nobody does what you did; nobody can. You invented it and it died with you.

Billy and I never found another safe house, either. Our hiding place died with you, too.

Madison, Wisconsin. We parked our vans by the lake with all the doors open and played new music for each other, Billy manning our CD player, Tina turning your quiet all the way up on yours. The three of us sat in the grass around your chair. No talking, because none of us ever talked while music was playing.

Your new song was untitled and never released. Now, to me, it's like a dream song. We watched the water while it played. I remember that it sounded like cellos, with your guitar tuned down and quadruple tracked. Hard to make out the words, the way you hummed and hollered 'em, but I'm not a words guy: I'm in for the full effect. A lovely slug to the gut when you were at your best. It sounded like how you and Tina changed a room just by entering it. Billy grabbed my hand on the grassy bank and we lay back to watch leaves and clouds.

The last chord rang out for a long time. I didn't want it to stop, even though at the time, I didn't know I'd never hear it again. Billy jumped up and started my newest song. "Your Dirty Answer." You half-smiled. I caught you from an odd angle, lying in the grass as I was. Smiling with the animated half of your leftist right-brained psychology, you stared out over the water, a stare as clear as the lake. Tina looked down at me, hard and soft at the same time. This was *our* sound, mine and Billy's. As ugly as yours was lovely, and still a slug to the gut. Poor Billy.

This was our clarity, though. Our church.

Our favorite thing was how you used to bash Tina on the thigh when you wanted her to appreciate something. We loved that nothing mattered to you until it had been absorbed by the Great and Powerful Tina, so you used the back of your hand to pound it into her eyes. Well, her legs.

We'd wait to see if a happening or a sentence or a joke or a thing mattered—got the thigh-whacking seal of approval— held our breaths until Tina stumbled away, laughing, bruised, and appreciative. Laughing and bruised and appreciative: probably the best anyone can do. That was a nice gift to give her.

Minneapolis. Big, ol' beautiful thee-ay-ter, full of exceptional junkie lumberjacks; a perfect night, after a perfect day spent in the botanical gardens. I named my new record after a little flower Tina found there: "Sunny Border Blue."

Billy, with a sideways glance at me: "Small packages."

Just as we were starting the first encore that night, I happened to look past you, back into the wings. We were about to begin, "Panic Pure," when I saw an enormous trunk with the word SNAKES printed on it in huge block letters. I stopped playing and pointed at it.

Glancing over your shoulder and peering into the darkness, you shook your head and grimaced. "We better play good."

Toronto. Us both fighting over Mary Margaret O'Hara, one of our favorite musicians. We each claimed her as a friend and told rivaling stories of our intimacy. Me: "She once gave me the coat off her back, literally. Just cuz I said I used to have one like it. She took it off and handed it to me in the snow. And it was really cold that day."

"She gave you perfume, too," added Billy.

Me: "Oh yeah, expensive perfume. Half a bottle full."

You: "Mary and I took a walk outside the Horseshoe once? And I nearly missed set time, we were having so much fun, laughin' and drunk as shit. She slipped on the ice and I caught her arm. She woulda fallen in the street and there was a big truck comin' . . . I saved her life."

Me: "Oh. Well. The perfume was from Barney's and it was freesia, my favorite flower because Billy used to bring them home to me in New York when we were dating and Mary *remembered* that."

Billy: "True story."

Me: "I still wear it every day. Also? She said I had beautiful skin."

You, steady and squinty: "She sang one of my songs once."

Me, steady and squinty back: "She sang backups on one of *my* songs."

Tina, rolling her eyes: "Can't you two just agree that all three of you are friends?"

"Well, sure!" you sing-songed, expansive. "We just wanna know which one of us she doesn't like."

Tina shook her head. "Y'all're third graders."

Duh-uh.

I guess in Canada, nobody owns a gun that isn't for shooting food, so they always let the whole goddamn audience into the dressing room after a show. Tonight the dressing room was a big, echoey, wooden space, like an old elementary school classroom. I could barely see you through the crowd as I fielded questions from college kids who swayed, gripping bottles of Moosehead. They all talked really fast. If I were that drunk, I'd talk *slow*, try to get it right. *Is that a Canadian thing, too? Talking fast when you're drunk?*

"I wrote down some of your lyrics tonight, in this notebook, but the words go by so quickly, especially when you *yell* 'em like that." This kid was wearing a few sweaters and like, three coats, and sweating profusely. He pushed the notebook into my hands. "I just wondered if you could read what I wrote down and tell me if I got 'em right. And if I didn't would it be okay to publish them as my own?" He looked at me with swimmy eyes. "And could you sign them?" He leaned toward me. "I think we have a lot in common. Also, one of *my* poems is in there. . . ."

I watched a bead of sweat pour down his forehead and join others glistening on his upper lip. "Why don't you take one of your coats off?" I asked him. He swayed and stared, confused.

"Excuse, me, Kristin?" Another sweaty guy very much like the first one jostled me from behind. He only had one coat on, so he was *less* sweaty, but his faculties were no more intact. He was so drunk, leaning into my personal space, I thought I might have to catch him. "I don't quite know how to put this, so I'll just say it." He talked even faster than the other guy, connecting every syllable as if he were speaking one, long German word. "I have also struggled with mental illness and I wonder if you think Western medicine's response to our conditions—to numb our ability to experience altered consciousness and the extremes of human emotion—has a detrimental effect on artistic expression. . . ." He had rehearsed this speech; his delivery was hypnotic.

Catching a glimpse of Mary Margaret across the room, I tried to excuse myself, but a little, round woman wearing a kind of muumuu grabbed my arm before I could leave. "I sew all my own clothes," she said meaningfully, then reached up and wrapped her arms around me in a teary bear hug. I was hugging her back lightly when, over her shoulder, I saw you next to Mary Margaret, engaged in rapt conversation. *Damn it!*

You caught my eye and waved, smug, as someone tapped me on the shoulder. I let go of the muumuu lady and turned around. An honest-to-god clown stood before me. A sad girl one. With tears drawn on her cheeks and an elaborate frown painted over her own elaborate frown. She wore a baggy, polka-dotted clown suit with an enormous neck ruffle and enormouser candy apple red clown shoes.

Alarmed, I stared wide-eyed as her bottom lip trembled. "I—I—I . . ." she began. Then her eyes filled with tears and she fell into my arms, sobbing. *This is a genuine psycho*, I thought. *All these drunk college kids are just self-absorbed. The lady who sews her own clothes is kind of a toss-up. But this clown? Is nuts.*

Muumuu lady, at a loss, reached around both of us, starting a group hug that a few other audience members joined. Through the hug, I caught a glimpse of you and Mary laughing, and I growled inside. Softly, in the clown's ear, mostly to get her off me, I asked, "Are you okay?"

She bounced up, completely recovered, pushing all the group huggers off each other awkwardly. They stumbled around for a second, then closed in again like buzzed jackals. "Yeah!" She grinned through her painted-on frown. "I waitress here during the week and I'm in clown college on the weekends. I just got out of class and wanted to catch the end of your show!" I stared at her, numb. "I'm a *sad* clown," she explained.

Sad clown. I thought about this. "You know who *loves* sad clowns?" I said, suddenly wildly enthusiastic. "Vic!" The clown chick gazed excitedly across the room at you monopolizing Mary Margaret. "Vic Chesnutt!" I announced, grabbing her hand, pushing past the circle of jackals and dragging her across the room through the staring crowd.

When we got to you, you twisted your head around as you tried to understand the girl clown. It didn't take you long. You squinted at me suspiciously. "This is Vic!" I told her pointedly. Then, to you: "I was just telling my new friend here how much you love clowns, Victor. Especially the sad kind of clown." You glared at me. "Hell, Vic is *himself* a sad clown, isn't that right? He was only recently referring to himself as such in London, England, while wearing a Rastafarian codpiece and—"

"How do you do?" you growled at the clown, looking darkly into my eyes.

"Excuse me," I said, smiling at both of them. "Mary!" I cried, throwing my arms around Mary Margaret and pulling her away so I could have her to myself. "I still smell like freesia, can you tell?"

We parked ourselves on a wooden pew against the wall, hiding from the noisy crowd. Me: "Is it a Canadian thing to talk fast when you're drunk?"

Her: "Oh, yeah, sure. We invented that."

She did a birdcall for me, then taught me how to do it and tried to give me her earrings, but I refused. I asked her if Vic had ever saved her life and she looked flummoxed. *I knew it.* "You mean metaphorically?"

"No, from a truck." She looked up in the air for the memory but didn't find it. I tried to smile at you but lost you in the crowd.

Mary said she'd played no music since some record executive told her that her voice made him sick. "God, people tell me that all the *time*, Mary," I said. "I take it as a compliment."

She shrugged and looked embarrassed, stared at the floor. "I guess I just didn't hear it that way."

I looked at the floor, too, where a couple of shiny red shoes had just appeared in front of us. Looking up, grim, I saw a hopeful clown frown. "Vic said you wanted to see me about something?" And then, to Mary, "He said to tell *you* the cab's here to take you guys to the Horseshoe." Mary put on her coat and I stood up with her.

The clown girl put on her saddest clown face and welled up again, gazing deeply into my eyes. "Vic said to tell you he's *really* sorry you aren't able to join them."

A few days off, at our house in New England. Billy and I lived on the island where I grew up; an odd amalgam of melancholy beaches and blue-collar grim that turned sun-shiny-scary every summer. Glossy tourists in sunglasses and bikinis'd replace the real people three months a year. But this was off-season: thickety time.

Billy took our doors off their hinges and stacked them on the back porch so you could wheel around our not handi-accessible old house, tacking a bed sheet to the bathroom door jamb. "This is your modesty curtain," he told you.

"When I take a whiz, it'll only be semi-private," you apologized.

"You need Greg Brady beads," I said.

Billy and I loved our little, old crappity house; had painted it all kinds off garish cartoon colors to celebrate it. We loved the cracked doorknobs and the smudgy windows, loved waking up to weather that had become *ours*, inherited from past grown-ups. Couldn't believe we owned A House.

But now we felt bad, watching you get stuck in corners, unable to navigate Victorian moldings, knowing you weren't ever gonna see the second floor where squirrels in the branches of trees *we owned* woke us up every morning.

So we took you to the beach. Well, you took us cuz you fit in your van better than you did in our car. But you wouldn't get out of the van, just called "See you in my dreams!" like you always did when you didn't wanna go somewhere with us. Then you watched Billy and me through the windshield . . . a little creepy. But you were a little creepy. And it was windy and gray, I didn't blame you; a cold beach isn't for everyone.

For some reason, we didn't take you to the good beach, we went to the lousy one. Maybe cuz the seashell pickins were better at the bad beach, but I couldn't coax you out onto the sand or even into the parking lot to find any. I wasn't thinking about wheels and sand, just thinking you were in a quiet way, happy to sit and stare. Happy to see us in your dreams instead of in real life.

The roaring wind blew hair into my eyes as Billy and I walked by the water, so I couldn't see you. Feeling guilty, like we'd just made you chauffeur us to the ocean, I asked him to check on you. "Vic okay?"

Billy was kicking a piece of seaweed along the sand studiously. Looking up, he peered into your windshield. "Vic looks extraordinarily peaceful."

Me: "Yeah, I thought so, too. Is he high?"

Billy: "Maybe. That's what most guys I know do in their vans at the beach."

So we brought you some seashells, which you placed politely on your dashboard, Kinder Surprise–style. On the way home, you didn't seem stoned, just thoughtful. Dreamy, almost. "What's up?" I asked you, climbing into the backseat. *Dreamy* is not generally a word any of us would've used to describe you.

"*Boo-ooze and vittles/the gentlest little/breakfast of slammers and wine*," you sang, starting the van and backing out of the parking lot sleepily.

"Oh," I said to Billy, grim. "He *is* high." Billy nodded. I leaned up and tapped you on the shoulder. "Making spaghetti tonight. The squid ink kind. Very cool. It's black."

"*A toke and a token/of comic, unspoken/truths that are already lies.*"

"There's real squid ink in it," I added.

You drove slowly, admiring the view, singing occasionally. "*Crowed like a rooster/unknown but to you, sir/for I am a drunken hog child.*"

"From squid," I turned to Billy. "Wonder who has to squeeze the ink outta the squid?"

Billy: "Yeah, is it like milking a cow? Or is that *it* for the squid . . . does he never work again?"

Nodding, I made a face. "I bet it's the second one."

Couldn't get you to talk without singing, so I quit trying; just watched the gray sky moving past, the damp grass, the island briars. Everything thorny and gnarled.

Pointing out to sea, I told Billy that before the hurricane of '38, there'd been a sort of carnival at the beach. "After the hurricane, people watched the ferris wheel float away." And I watched him stare out the window after it for the longest time, stare at the ghost of a ferris wheel as it disappeared.

A motel in Raleigh, North Carolina. Billy and I lay in bed, watching *Holiday* and ignoring Katharine Hepburn and Cary Grant. We only had eyes for Edward Everett Horton and Jean Dixon, who played giggly, middle-aged professors. They lived in front of their fireplace in armchairs as far as we could tell . . . forever friends and lovers, forever telling time by the clock on the mantelpiece, for no other reason than that numbers are nice. No time in heaven, see. Clouds around the whole scene: their apartment building, their lives. A lovely limbo.

"That's us," said Billy.

"That's us," I agreed. And there was no time in that hotel room, even though numbers are nice.

Your house in Athens, Georgia. Our Safe House: we knew it by heart, having heard it in your songs, then crashing here time and again when we couldn't face the outside world. Such a hiding place. Our futon off the back porch, next to the kitchen. The window at the foot of our bed looked out onto nothing, but I loved to look out of it. A parking place. "Fazing and gazing," Billy called it one morning while we waited for your kettle to boil. He was trying not to judge me for doing nothing, I guess, making it sound languid. Billy could fix anything.

I'd been droning on about the softness of Georgia; told him that having been born into its kindness, it had become a part of me or some shit . . . trying to spin doormat as warmth. So, really, I was looking for peace out the window; tearing up the air with frantic eyes, looking to dredge up some tenderness and wear it as my own. The Georgia air—same as the air everywhere else—called my bullshit.

Billy was still in bed, unable to shake off the effects of a sleeping pill Tina'd called "gentle" (this was not the case . . . maybe us southern women just *lie*) and an awful cheerleader drink she'd been pushing on us since we got in the day before. Sprite and . . . like, rum or something. As a rule, you were either drinking heavily or prevented from drinking, and this was a prevented-from-drinking time, so you watched us down this stuff with a smirk on your face. I couldn't finish mine, but Tina and Billy had had a few of 'em. Just cuz Sprite and rum is funny, I think. Not real funny the next morning, though. Billy's arm was across his forehead and his tongue sounded thickened. "Would. Like. To. Barf," he mumbled.

"I think Tina might be . . . hard," I said thoughtfully. "Like, the bitchin' kind of hard. We maybe shouldn't try to keep up with her."

I was fuzzy, too, but just tour fuzzy. Compromised enough to study Billy—his arm covering his face—and see him clearly. I had to admit, we were still Lost in Spain. Reluctantly, I unfolded the crumpled snapshot from my limbic photo album: he was a complete whole, but with pieces missing. *How can this be?* There were parts of him that . . . weren't for me. He held a hammer in one hand, a blindfold in the other, kept me safe. But also scared and in the dark. *Maybe all safety nets are full of holes.*

I was stuffing the snapshot back through a tour crack in my skull when the kettle whistled. I spun around the corner to grab it before it woke y'all, but you were sitting silently in the kitchen, already looking at me. *Yikes.*

"Tina is hard," you agreed.

I turned the flame down under the kettle and the whistle died. "She seems so soft."

You nodded and faze-gazed out the window.

Really, we were all four of us hard in our own way. Uneasy. That's why I had to hope and wish and pray that our moments and our muscles'd let us go limp. Someday. Just get easy cuz we'd . . . had such a hard time. Fighting and flying.

III. GO OUTSIDE AND LOOK AT THE MOON

The first time you died, I was sitting in your recording studio in Nashville, breathing in a southern breeze and talking dumb shit about night bark smelling better in the south: different and more *right*. "Look, I brought you a six-pack. Want a beer?" I held one out.

"Can't, not allowed."

"Again? Whadja do *this* time?"

You shrugged. Must've been bad. "Night bark?"

"Can *I* drink it? Yeah, night bark."

You drooped a little, drained. "You want the whole six-pack?"

"No, just this one."

"Par-tay," you croaked. "Cuz I was adopted, I always thought I'd have some kinda, I dunno, *instinctive associations* of . . . elsewhere. Florida night bark never spoke to me, though."

"Florida's right down there," I said, pointing. "The bark isn't too different. Whatsa matter with your voice?"

"Cold. Been singin' . . ."

"You coulda had roots in the Ukraine or something. Maybe you haven't yet come across the right trees."

You nodded. "It'd be nice to find out that at our core is not our failings." Drowsy with maybe, cold medicine. I hoped it was cold medicine. "That we're mostly concerned with trees. And how they smell." Your hoarse voice made you sound exhausted, like you'd surrendered.

"'Course!" I think I might've sounded gleeful. Sorry. Nobody likes me gleeful, it's annoying. "When you're a baby, you haven't failed yet."

You gritted your teeth. "There has to be a song that triggers a core response." This was painful for you.

"Mmmmmaybe." You aren't supposed to *plan* songs. I looked into your coffee cup. Ugly granules of your instant crap, floating in cold water. "You want something better to drink? I mean, I know not a beer, but they probly have tea here . . . for your cold."

Pain, for real: "We could write a song that everybody understood, or at least anybody could understand. We could do that."

"Don't care about that," I shrugged. I cared that you cared, but I didn't care. We'd been over this and over this: you were tasked with complexity of expression, which is a big, fat bummer and we're sorry as hell and all that, but self-parody is a sad road. "Don't you dare imitate a watered-down version of your berserkness. I swear to god, if you suck, you might as well be dead. You'll be dead to *me*, anyway."

"We could do it *together*." Mad-scientist glint in your eye. Ugly. "How are we helping if we alienate people with all this pretense of art?"

"What? Faking it is pretentious." You knew this. "Manipulative." You *knew* this. "And don't say 'art.'" I watched you cough. The coughs bent you over and left you that way, in sort of a wheezing posture, like a very old man. "So tell me about this song you're recording."

"It's gay," you sighed, grim.

"Please stop calling things gay."

Bored, piercing look. "It's a song about a poem about a painting."

"Oh. Well . . . I'm sure it's very nice." I glanced into the corner of the room, where guinea pigs were gurgling and snuffling around a converted fish tank. Your studio had guinea pigs in it. Mine had horses.

"We gotta edit is all." You weren't stopping. "Take out the weird." Greasy and unwashed, you seemed impure. You were always greasy and unwashed, but I'd thought a heart of gold lay beneath the coating of grime. Tonight, you were a smudgy window; dirty old pigeon flutter the only view. "We could make a record of pared-down inspiration that moved *everybody*." You knew how this sounded, so you added a spin: "That'd be the commie thing to do."

"Pared down? That's what selling out *is*. It's not your mission." What happened to you? What the hell orgasm is in selling out? What about unhappy accidents? Mutations? "Jesus, Vic, don't *suck*. We can make a record together, but . . . you know . . . let's make a *good* record."

"I can't, I'm broke." You drank those awful brown granules floating in cold water.

To me, your pristine wings began to disintegrate then, feather by feather, graying and cruddy. A knock on the door and my husband stood on the doorstep in the rain, looking clean and strong. Billy hurt, Billy was broke, but he was a clean window. I drained my beer, poked a finger into the guinea pigs' cage, and left with him, as you glided back into the control room to try and control music.

Christmas Eve. Cell phone scrunched between my ear and shoulder, I wrapped Christmas presents on the floor of my bright orange practice space while you told me how it felt to be stuck in an elevator in Athens.

"I don't understand." Holding some penguins-in-Santa-hats wrapping paper in place with my thumb, I searched in vain for the tape. "You're in an elevator *now*?"

"Were you even listening?" you squawked.

I lifted a roll of paper and pushed some gifts aside, found the scissors but not the tape. "And you're still trapped?"

"Hell-*o*-o!" You sounded happy *and* pissed off. Actually, you always sounded happy and pissed off.

"What am *I* supposed to do? You're in Athens. Why don't you call the Athens fire department or something?"

"I dunno . . . thought you might care. Or think it was funny." You blew into the phone. "Or have an idea that'd get me the fuck out of here."

"Ah-ha!"

"What?"

I sighed happily. "Found the tape."

"Found the what?"

"Tape. It's Christmas Eve." I switched my phone to the other ear. "Nothing. I've never been trapped in an elevator before, I've only seen it happen in movies and they usually climb out through an opening in the ceiling."

"I'm lookin' up," you narrated. "Ain't no hole in the ceiling."

"Shoot. You want me to call somebody for you?"

"God, you're retarded. I-am-speaking-to-you-on-a-tele-phone."

Sticking a bow over a penguin's face, I grabbed the next gift and some silver wrapping paper. "Oh, yeah. Where's Tina? Why don't you call her instead of me? She lives in your house, she could come . . . rescue you."

"I'm *in* my house. This is my own elevator I'm stuck in."

My mouth fell open. "You got an *elevator*? In your *house*? Coooooool!"

"It was cool at first. Now I'm not so into it." There was a shuffling noise. "There *might* be an opening up there, now that I look. My eyes are still adjusting to the dark."

"It's dark in there? Christ."

". . . but I don't see me getting to it so easy. Jimmyin' the door seems like a better way to go."

Holy shit. "So you're really stuck?"

[audible sigh]

". . . in an elevator?"

[louder sigh]

". . . that you *own*?"

[silence]

Lost the tape again. "But where does it go? I mean, where were you going when you got on it? You don't have a second floor."

"'Course I do."

I held the silver wrapping paper down with my left hand while I felt around for the tape with my right, mentally walking through Vic and Tina's house. "No. You don't." Found the tape: *yes!*

"You just never seen it cuz you couldn't get to it before. I had a staircase put in so you could get to it."

"You had stairs put in? You hate stairs." I put a gold bow on the silver present and started on another.

"Yep. That's why I had this goddamn elevator put in."

"I still think that's pretty cool."

More shuffling. "Yeah. Thanks." A loud clatter. Then silence.

"Vic?" Muffled banging. "*Vic?*!"

Shuffling. "Shut up. I just dropped my phone."

"Oh. Jesus." I suddenly realized that you were actually trapped in an elevator. "What if you run out of air? Or die of dehydration? What if the next time I go to your house, you're a skeleton in a chair covered in cobwebs and shit . . . is it cold?"

"'Course it's cold, it's winter," you grumbled, then guffawed into the phone so loud, it distorted. "Loved your Christmas card! I spat my cawfee, I was laughin' so hard!"

"Glad you liked it. When's Tina get home?"

"She's not."

"She's not what?"

Long pause. "Comin' home."

". . . no?"

Longer pause. "Nope."

I grabbed a book and stuffed it into a gift bag. "Why not?"

"Tina ain't gettin' home."

This meant nothing. Cutting a long piece of wrapping paper covered in ludicrous junkie-like Santa faces, I let the phone slip off my shoulder. "Whaddya mean? Where'd she go?"

"What?"

"What-did-you-do-with-your-wife?

Even longer pause. "She's at her boyfriend's house."

I chuckled. "Who?" Holding up the swath of colored paper, I stared into a junkie Santa's eyes. "What does *that* mean?"

"We got a divorce." You said this like you were telling me that you guys got a dog.

I froze, me and junkie Santa staring at each other. *This doesn't happen.* "Huh?"

"We were fightin' a lot."

"Vic." I let the wrapping paper fall to the floor. "You don't divorce Tina Chesnutt."

"Naw, but ya do divorce Vic Chesnutt. He's a dickhead."

I didn't know what to say. I don't think I said anything for a long time; we just sat there breathing into our cell phones at each other. You'd lost your reason to live. Lost your pain-killer. "I'm . . ." What the fuck *do* you say? "I'm so sorry."

"Yeah." Still nothing to say.

Our lives as two couples didn't exactly flash before my eyes, I just got stuck in one memory: laughing over tiny farm eggs in a midwestern diner. Tina's bleary shining as she admired the orange yolks. "These eggs came from *chickens*," I told her, "just like the ones in Ireland." I studied them. "Or maybe ducks."

You guys told us about your trip to Mexico and the little girl who'd carried a coatimundi over to your van, tried to get you to buy it. When you refused, she dragged the coatimundi back to her mother, sullen, while the mother pointed and laughed. "You have failed to sell . . ." you announced, pointing accusingly, ". . . the coatimundi!" I can't tell you how this sentence stuck in our heads. I guess it got stuck there because no one else had ever said it before. Certainly not in exactly that way. Not with sixteen syllables.

Our tiny, sunny eggs got colder and clammier. We found out that the one thing we all had in common growing up was that our families thought we were gay. "Interesting," Tina squinted.

You nodded. "It's cuz we're great."

"Balanced?" I asked and Billy nodded. "We're a new kind of people," he said.

Tina: "So's everybody we like."

You: "I'm so straight, it's *sad*."

Me: "I'm pretty sad that I'm straight. I think it shows a lack of imagination."

A look from Billy. He told us that when he was a teenager, his parents had asked him if he was gay and he'd told them no. His mother: "But if you *were* gay, you'd tell us, right?" His answer? "No."

So we were all four of us hard, yet balanced. In that limbic limbo of extremes pulling at each other, fighting for control of our heart monitors, the needles jumping and twitching. *It'll be okay*. We had each other. Alone together, etc.

Then, for some reason, over his rye toast, Billy began talking casually about my deep unworthiness. Heart monitor twitching, my white knuckles gripped the paper napkin on my lap, but Billy was . . . easy. No hammer, no blindfold, didn't whip his wedding ring across the room or anything. It was a kindness on his part.

Billy's mouth fell open when he told you guys I felt like the devil's daughter. My mouth fell open, too. I'd been so sure my dirty was gonna lose him, push him away, send him packing for a gooder woman. And there he was *on my side*, of all things. "It's just the songs," I stuttered, embarrassed. "They're so . . . dark. Evil-ugly."

"Not at *all*!" you breathed in protest and Tina sent me soft waves across the table, over half-empty ramekins of grape jelly. "I feel ugly, Vic feels evil," she said. "You are not alone."

And Billy, smiling: "I'm evil *and* ugly. None of us is alone."

Lost in Santa Junkie's insane eyes, buried under a pile of wrapping paper, I leaned back against the bright orange wall of my practice space, so far away from that diner. *None of us is alone* is what the four of us found out together. It had all been so . . . fun. *How will you be happy now?*

I still didn't know what to say. Didn't want to leave that diner memory, with the highway in front and fields in the back, patches of snow in dry straw, real chicken-ducks somewhere, old syrup in the carpet, burned coffee in our stained cups. I wanted to get off the phone with you and call Tina, but that made no sense. You and Tina were the same in my mind. "Are you okay?" It was all I could think to ask.

"Play a show with me." You sounded weak. You'd sounded a lot of things before, but never weak. "Then I'll be okay."

Jesus. "Anything." I didn't see how on earth you were ever gonna be okay again, though.

"Promise?" you pleaded. Bitch Chesnutt pleading. Not something I ever wanted to hear.

"Yeah, sure. And let's make that record together. But . . . don't—"

I heard a buzzing from your end. "Hey, the electricity's back on! I'm free! Goin' to the second floor now. See ya."

"*That's* why it was dark and cold and you were stuck? The power was out?"

"It is always dark and it is always cold and I am always stuck," you giggled. Giggling?? *You are losing your shit*, I thought, *you are bonkers.* Your laughter stopped short. "I shouldn't have to get stuck in a elevator for you to figure *that* out."

I leaned back against the orange wall, my feet in a pile of silver Christmas detritus. "Vic. Please decide that that's bullshit. You can do any fucking thing you want."

You laughed bitterly. "Oh yeah? What should I do first?"

I sighed. "I don't wanna be melodramatic, but . . . live?"

"Yeah, right. This is me, to me: 'Just gimme a reason, gimme a fucking reason.'"

"Well, I *know.* That's why I said that."

"Look, I need both hands to get off this elevator, so I gotta go."

I really didn't wanna let you go. This is what people meant when they said we were gonna lose you. This is how they felt when they didn't wanna let you go. But saving you wasn't my job, wasn't in the cards. "Merry Christmas, Vic."

"Merry Christmas, Kristin." You hung up and, I guess, glided out onto your mysterious second floor.

Then I had a terrible thought. Dialed the cell phone as quickly as I could. You let it ring and ring. Went to voice mail. You're outgoing message was, "Fuck off." I waited for the beep. "Answer the phone, dickhead," I said, then hung up and waited.

I was staring at your Christmas card, which I'd taped to the wall of my practice space: a pencil drawing of a can of tomatoes, when my cell phone rang. "What?" you squealed. "I'm *busy*."

"God, you sound like my grandma. It's uncanny."

"What-do-you-want?"

"Don't suck."

"Huh?"

"Don't water down your berserk, don't suck."

You, deeply offended: "Don't *suck*?"

"I mean it. We've been through this. I knew you weren't listening. Listen *now*."

You loved that free fall so much. The one that terrified me, that haunted me at four a.m., that lost me my mind and my friends and Billy until I could snap the fuck out of it again. Now we both knew you were willing to fake that fall. Which'd never work cuz your genius wasn't something

Christmas card from Vic.

you were, it was something that drove you around. It chauffeured you to hell and back, to heaven and back, to your old neighborhood, to Spanish moss, pushed you out onto thin ice, wherever it needed you to go for the next cliff dive.

Then your genius'd drive you home, open its mean limo doors and toss you out onto your lawn, throwing your new song out with you, rolling it across the yard, where you'd snatch it up cuz it was precious. The noise that pain makes is beautiful when it's set to music. The noise joy makes is *more* beautiful, but it was all still gross, what we did. And you loved it. I tumbled off the edges of cliffs, slipped and fell, clawing at the dirt, but you were braver than me. You *loved* cliff diving. You loved it so much that if the limo didn't show up, you were willing to build your own cliff and try to fly off it: a sandcastle rather than a precipice. Gravity is cruel, but reliable. Shifting sand less so.

"Okay. You neither." Sober. "Don't suck."

"And don't die," I added quickly.

"Don't suck, don't die," you repeated. "Deal?"

"Deal." I listened to your silence to hear if it was real. "Okay."

"Lies upon lies and lies back." Your creepy grandma voice. "Lie back for more lies. See you in my dreams!" *Click*.

In Tucson, we played the show I'd promised you, at the Hotel Congress, with Howe Gelb and John Doe. You were not waiting on the sidewalk when we got there. Billy and I checked into our room—our very warm room. Felt like we were in *Paper Moon*. The Hotel Congress is without modern amenities, meaning, it is real and it is going-back-in-time and it is perfect. Our mushy, rainy winter-spring bodies were sucking up the dry Sonoran air, balancing. "I think my skin is smaller," Billy said, pinching his arm.

"I'm gonna go find Vic," I told him, "wanna come?"

Stare. "Nope."

So I wandered the halls and grounds alone, looking for you, but you'd taken off somewhere, as usual. I met some desert people, took a picture of an interesting cactus, bought a couple iced coffees, but no James Victor Chesnutt. When I got back to our room, Billy was wearing a towel, his hair wet and messy. "Shower doesn't work," he announced.

"How'd you get wet?"

He looked at me, blank, and picked up the phone *as it rang*.

"How did you do that?" I hissed at him, handing him his coffee. He was sometimes a little not human. Like, he didn't need to eat. Not like the rest of us do; not to live. He only ate for fun. And he didn't need to breathe, either. That was real weird. Suspect, though I wouldn't know what to suspect.

Billy shrugged and held out the receiver. Howe yelled, "HELLO!" all Howey. Nobody can do Howe but Howe; he's so goddamn Howe, even compressed by an old telephone receiver from the seventies. East-west, north-south, urban-desert, art-cowboy, scattered, buckshot-shooting, always looks like he's thinking about something else. "Helping Vic find a place to live!" he shouted and Billy repeated it for my benefit: "He's helping Vic find a place to live."

"I heard. A place to live?"

"A place to live?" Billy asked Howe and held out the receiver to me again.

Then you squealed in the background, a little, tiny grandma, "Help, Billy! Help, Kristin! Help meeeeeeee . . ."

"On our way!" Billy called, grabbing the car keys.

We found you in an empty adobe, down the street from Howe's bright blue house, parked in the echoey living room, staring. Howe announced us. "The man of the hour! And the woman we've been waiting for! Tell us if these curtains are tacky or shabby chic?"

"For we are but men and therefore barbarians," you added.

I smiled. "I don't know from curtains . . ."

"Told you she wasn't a woman," you muttered to Howe, but held out your arms to me, anyway. You didn't look divorced, you looked exactly the same, except for a Tina-shaped black hole beside you. Also, when I hugged you, you felt brittle.

"You feel brittle," you said to me, concerned.

I nodded. "So do you."

"I got a divorce, what'd you get?"

"A liver infection."

Your Little Rascals face. "Me, too! Almost died."

"Me, too! I think. Worst pain I've ever felt."

"I don't feel pain," you said offhandedly.

Right. I forgot. "I did a photo shoot for the new record?" I babbled. "With that liver infection? And they had to turn me upside down before I looked like myself."

Beat. "They turned you upside down?"

"Well, sideways. And then I got my face back."

Squint. "What did your face look like before?"

"Crooked. I saw some of the pictures. My eyes were on wrong and I was kind of a funny color, so they had to put

different makeup on me. Gave me pink cheeks and new lips."
I was chatty, uncomfortable, made you suspicious. But you
minus Tina was . . . what? I didn't know yet. "Well, they always give me new lips cuz mine are on wrong—"

"I know."

"Nothing they could do about my eyes being on wrong,
though, so they turned me upside down."

"Sideways."

I glanced at you to see if you were making fun of me, but
you actually looked extra kind.

"Yeah, sideways. I'll show you the pictures."

"You do that." And you said it like you meant it, for once.
"What'd they do to your fucked-up lips?"

I covered my mouth and spoke through my hand. "Can
you tell they're fucked up?"

"Yeah, they're way off." You nodded emphatically, "One
of 'em is, anyway. The top one. Yer about as ugly as that old
donut dumpster dog. In the lips."

"Six-Million-Dollar-Man-Steve-Austin?"

"Lee Majors."

I nodded, back in time for a moment. "I remember him."
I didn't really, though. I remember that there was a three-
legged dog and a donut, but I saw only the cutting wind of
Billy's green stare. Got lost in it for a minute; a disconcert-
ingly right place to be, like a mountaintop, a manic ocean.
Shook it off.

Pulling my top lip out to illustrate, I shifted it to the left
and pressed it into place. "It's supposed to be over here, so
that's where they draw it on." I wiped my fingers on my shirt

to get the spit off. "And then when I talk, a big hole opens up in my face that's only partially surrounded by lips."

For a son of a bitch, you radiated kindness. "Keep tellin' you not to do that."

"Talk? Yeah, I know." Out the window was a saguaro wearing white flowers which snapped in the hot wind.

Maybe you were an angel, I don't know. You only sometimes acted like one.

Howe and Billy wandered into the kitchen to open the cabinets, for some reason. Slammed 'em all open, then shut. "We found Hot Wheels!" Billy called to us, excited. Put Howe and Billy together and they turned six; it was crazy. And fun. You didn't do that and you *really* needed to. You turned six sometimes, but not in a fun way; in a James-Victor-Chesnutt-shoots-trees-'til-they-fall-down way.

"Hot Wheels!" you echoed back.

"You're moving to Tucson?" I asked you, suddenly remembering what we were doing in that empty house.

"Depends," you shrugged. "If those curtains are tacky or shabby chic."

"Cuz of the divorce?"

"Nah. Yeah. Naw. I had to get outta town." You wheeled over to the bedroom and peered in. "Pain killers. Pain and killers. Painkillers. Kristin. Let's get some tequila."

What the? It was like a dream in that adobe. "Okay. So . . . drinking again?"

"So nuthin'. *Hell*, yeah." You looked mad and dazed. "Every hurt heals with scar tissue."

Unless it doesn't heal.

You, singing: *"I was a dick/I had to git."* You, to the ceiling: *"What is that sick . . . ly . . . sweet. Kristin?"*

So you're nuts now. "Yeah?"

"Nuthin'."

"Vic. Who . . ." I cleared my throat carefully. "Who left whom?"

"I did it!" Proudly. Your bony wings spread out behind your wheelchair, like they were gonna lift you off the ground, but . . . they couldn't anymore. They were a useless memory of wings.

"You left Tina?"

"I pushed her out the door!" you announced. There was the shame. Somebody accuses you of stealing a prop sheep with a huge vagina and you're *proud*, but now I knew why. Inside the ego bubble we could reach out and pop with one finger floated a personality *made* of shame. You were built on a foundation of humiliation and that disappeared an entire woman. "Pursuit of happiness," you spat.

Happiness? *Do unto others,* I thought, but couldn't say it out loud. Your bubble was ugly and I didn't wanna be anywhere near it, didn't wanna talk to it. I slumped against the wall, just to get a few inches farther away from you.

"Shoved her out. Pretty sure she hates me now." You turned love into hate? If there was a devil, isn't that what he would do?

At this point, gravity began to increase. Becoming more and more dense, we both slowed way down. I weighed a thousand pounds and so did my head. Scraping your wheels across the floor, you dragged yourself away angrily, muttering something I couldn't hear. My thinking fuzzy, my thoughts heavy, I tried to imagine what could transpire in a psychology to make it push *that* woman out any door. But the door to your beautiful house? That you built together? Tina carried your guitar *and* your suitcase. She was . . . Tina. She stared down into the chasms of your comas, for christ sake.

You were a lucky dickhead. You married gold and resented its shining. Could've worn it proudly, but instead, jealous, you threw it out the window.

I could feel the anger swelling, unchecked. Cut it off at the kneecaps because you were in hell. A hell you built, maybe, but it still wasn't where I wanted you to be. Couldn't help Tina from out here in an empty adobe in Tucson, so I breathed away my pissed off and followed you through yours, through the whitewashed rooms, in slow motion. "No stairs," I observed. "That's good, right?"

"Too many doors. Doors have gotta come down. I like whizzin' in plain sight."

"Never got the Greg Brady beads, huh?" You placed both your hands in the doorframe as if you were measuring for beads. "You're moving to Tucson?" I asked, tired. "How come you're moving to Tucson?"

You shrugged. "Don't got nuthin' else to do."

I sat on the bare floor, giving up. You were so close to Lost Cause. Such an old story. Moldy story. *God, make up something better*. Move on. "You could . . . not suck and die."

Nodding soberly, you said softly. "Don't suck, don't die. Noted. However . . ." Over my head, you squinted out the window into glaring desert sun. "I am not made of wood." This tickled your brain tongue, so you found a melody for it. "I . . ." Four syllables, no lie. "*Am not made of wood.*"

Me: "Vic, death is boring." You ignored this.

Howe and Billy came in from the kitchen as your voice echoed through the empty house. Both men held crappy-pretty little Matchbox cars in their outstretched hands, shiny blue and matte red, chipped paint. Both men glowed with health and electricity, both men were wildly okay. Instinctively, I moved toward them and away from you.

You shook your mangy wings, and grayish feathers floated to the polished wooden floor. "*I am not made of wood,*" you sang again. I'd seen you fly and here you were, dissipating. Fallen, but not in free fall: in misery, but still singing. "*I am not a good . . . man.*"

No, not always. But you were maybe a good angel.

As the audience was calling for the last encore that night, we all stood side of stage, under more stars than there could possibly be. Night deserts are crazy. The wind blows *indigo* or something. Thin and bone-sucking dry, yet thick with minerals. Howe had some very Howe idea about what we should all play together. None of us other musicians could follow it, though; we kept tilting our heads and looking at each other and interrupting to say, "Wait" or "Hold on," while Howe spoke in short, drunken phrases, *as we were stepping onto the stage.* "A standard," he said vaguely, and leaned back. Way back, like he was gonna fall over, then righted himself with a sly smile.

You: "A what?"

Howe: "In G minor, then we drop down to B-flat major and into a Giant Sand instrumental."

Me: "That none of us know."

You: "*What* standard?"

Howe: "It doesn't matter! That's the beauty of it."

You: "Aw, hell."

John Doe blanched. "I'll play tambourine . . ."

Howe just laughed.

Me: "Howe? No." And he laughed again, ran out waving to the crowd, all Howe-cool while the three of us slunk out behind him, already ashamed of mistakes we hadn't yet made. Howe picked a capo off his amp and wrapped it around the neck of my guitar. "Problem solved!"

"No, it isn't," I complained while the audience clapped. "I still don't know standards or Giant Sand instrumentals. Besides, don't you have to tell us *which* standard we're supposed to be playing?"

Howe laughed. "I told you, it doesn't matter! That's the beauty of it!"

You: "That is not what 'beauty' means."

Me: "I don't do capos, anyway. Don't believe in 'em."

The crowd stopped clapping and just watched us fumble around. John put on his bass, smiling, but looked close to tears: "Where's my tambourine?" he hissed through his teeth.

Howe began playing and so did we. And goddamnit, he was right, it didn't matter. That was the beauty of a drunk Howe and that *is* what "beauty" means. I stared out into the growing darkness, the candle flames flapping back and forth in that clean wind. Found Billy's silhouette, watched a couple hundred Converse All Stars under tables, tapping in long shadows.

You cocked your head at me while we played and I bent down to hear what you had to say. "Sometimes?" you shouted into my ear over the amps. "Just every now and then . . ."

Sounded so much better when you said it than when I thought it. Settled me. Cuz you'd been so dark that day, but I figured only an angel can read people's minds.

After the show, I sat on Billy's lap and our friends gathered around us in the candlelight. You gliding up. John and Howe scratching chairs across the ground, all smiles. The Tucson indigo around us was impenetrable, the murmuring people soft and misty. Desert gentleness, like a wide open cave: a different kind of safety. *Huh.* Just for a minute, just for tonight. And our timeless catacomb of a Paper Moon hotel room waiting, warm and dry, its hot sheets lonely enough for the two of us to feel safe.

The next morning, we ate breakfast in the hotel, a big group of us. Waves of laughter, coffee-fueled commotion. I wore a wife beater and Howe's hat, which he said looked better on me than him, so I smashed it down over my eyebrows to look extra retarded. For some reason, I remember that the floor was made of pennies and Howe's T-shirt was the color of chocolate milk. He told us that the Gulf War was the color of chocolate milk, which made us all pause for a second and stare off, picturing that.

Tina was missing and I missed her. Couldn't imagine how much *you* missed her. I mean, really, couldn't even imagine. Tried. Couldn't. Pigeons pecked around the tables outside, eating soggy toast crumbs and chunks of a cinnamon roll a toddler whipped across the courtyard at them. "Vegan confections!" you announced. "Killing the pigeons . . ." and this became a song again, all these years later. It was now merely a soundtrack we all ignored. Background noise.

Billy and Howe had some screaming match going on; imitating howler monkeys, I think. Billy does a wicked howler monkey. I held his hand under the table and could feel vibrating screams through it. Thing is, he was gonna win and Howe didn't know this. Billy always won, for one thing, but also, like I said, he didn't have to breathe. I'd sometimes find him at the bottom of pools, just lying there, no bubbles popping at the surface. An unusual skill. His hand felt so alive in mine, coursing with chemistry and noise, muscle fibers twitching . . . when the Sad Peter Pan across the table had become a puzzle. One with broken and missing pieces. Hard to tell what your puzzle was supposed to have been a picture of that morning.

I let go of Billy's hand for a minute to lean across the table and jab a fork into your pancakes, wake you up. The fork stood up straight, as if it were lodged in cement. You fashioned a little paper hat for it out of your napkin, singing your old English pigeon song.

I once was a waffler
A tea drinking scofflaw

A murderer of first degree
I fed British pigeons
Carrot confections
And watched them fall into the sea.

Staring at you under the brim of Howe's hat, warily: "There was only the one pigeon and he didn't fall into any sea . . . a *fountain* maybe."

Removing the paper hat from your fork, you carefully cut a triangle out of one of the pancakes and studied it in the air. "Sea of humanity. Sea of pigeon-manity. Manitees in the sea."

"Tourette's is kicking in again." *Where's Tina?* I thought. *She should be here.* 1. She deserves to be here. 2. Nobody is taking care of you. 3. You aren't funny anymore.

Monkey hooting drowned out whatever you said next. I squinted through the noise. "Huh?"

"Nothing. I wonder if it'd kill *me*, too." Catching my eye over the pancake triangle, you said, "Death by vegan confection is not a bad way to go."

"'Course it is . . . Nothing sadder than an embarrassing death. Imagine: 'Vic Chesnutt Killed by Carrot Cake.' Jesus. After all you've done. You would be so sad and dead. Missed opportunity."

"Don't eat carrot cake anyway; don't do allspice shit anymore."

I took a sip of coffee, bored, turned toward the howling. You hated to bore, hated to be turned away from. "Death by pancake," you threatened.

"Uh-uh. Even dumber. Dumbest death ever. You'd get points for *that*, I guess: Dumbest Death Ever."

Shoving the bite of pancake in your mouth, you chewed at me. "Felled by a microbe is pretty dumb."

"No way, man. *Mystery Disease*." I grabbed Billy's hand again to feel what *life* was like. You and death . . . *christ*. "Death by quagga. Brown reverse zebra, only two left. Sent some guy in to get a sperm sample at the London Zoo? Carried him out in a body bag. True story. I also knew a guy who cut off his head. He played a lobster monster in a movie and then cut off his own head. I don't know how you do that, but he did it. Nice guy, too." You stared. "Also a true story."

Nodding, you gave up on your pancake and put your fork down decisively. "Helium."

"Suit of armor on a golf course in an electrical storm."

"The bends."

"Hantavirus."

"Stingray through the heart."

I winced. "Geez. You win."

"For I am the Victor!"

At the same moment, Billy won the howler monkey contest. Even the waitress was impressed. He can yell real loud. "He's from New York," I told her, smiling proudly up at my giant. But when I turned back to smile at you, your eyes were dead; turned around, looking at the inside of your skull. I'd seen that in lotsa folks. A bad sign, in my experience. A symptom, a harbinger. Hate harbingers. "Hot Seat": *Pretty soon I know I'll do/precisely what I wanted not to do.*

"Vic," I said sadly, to wake you up, and your red eyes and filthy wings fluttered back onto this plane.

Racing up to your van as you pulled out of Howe's dusty driveway, I slapped the side of it like you would a horse. "Hey!"

You stopped but wouldn't look at me. *What the fuck?* "James Victor? Where are you going?" I threw a CD into the passenger window. "That's my new band, Fifty Foot Wave."

"Okay," you said to the windshield.

"Where you going? I thought you were moving to Tucson."

"Nope. Curtains were below par."

Climbing into the van, I studied you. Got a sideways glance, nothing else. "Whatsa matter?"

"Tired." Still talking to the windshield. "No sleep."

"Aw, I'm sorry." And I was. I cared. Nobody cares. "How come?"

Then you faced me with all the fury you had and used those blue discs of yours to burn holes into me and shook your shoulders like you wanted to shake mine and threw your torso across the car and into the gear shift as if you wanted to throw *me* across the car and impale me on your gear shift and you screamed huge and mean right into my kinda small, fairly friendly face: "*I GOT A DI-VO-RCE*!!" And divorce had three syllables, if not four, of course.

This was all the opposite of that diner morning on a midwestern highway. Who knows what will sparkle on this earth?

DON'T SUCK, DON'T DIE

Half-empty ramekins of grape jelly and runnels of snow. All of it gone.

I tried to imagine the agony of losing an elaborate human like Tina Chesnutt. You had no painkiller any more, no reason to live. I knew that'd be a chasm, but I could barely peer down into it. And there you were, free-falling. You were finally in a plummet you hated; nothing anyone could do to help. Sort of like what happened to Tina whenever you left her to go on one of your comas.

I tried to picture Billy removing his heart from our picture, but, careful fingertips out, I walked into a wall. Love is a shaky darkness maybe, but we can't help loving; that's the point. Love just *is*.

For you, love was, and then it was not.

You leaned back and sighed because your personal hurricane was over for the moment. Mine was still going on—I'd never let you yell at me before—but it had way more to do with you than me. So I gave it to you, didn't take it with me. Maybe if I had, I would've understood the next few years, but I didn't. I left that particular hurricane a dust devil, hovering over the gear shift in your van, obscuring the view out your windshield which had been a happy place and which was now a doomed undercurrent. You saw our beautiful lousy beach through that windshield, saw fat hover truckers through that windshield, ate a cinnamon Jolly Rancher in the driver's seat, Tina at your side. But now, in the bright Sonoran desert, your story had shifted into the shadows and your view—your perspective—joined it there.

Deciding that I'd witnessed a moment of panic and fury, not a personality of panic and fury, I shook it off and unfolded the newspaper under my left arm. "Well, you aren't gonna believe this." I spread the paper out on the dashboard and jabbed a finger at a black-and-white photo of a man in safari shorts. "Check it out. Steve Irwin. The croc hunter? Killed by a *stingray to the heart*. Can you fucking believe it?"

Blank stare.

"You killed him with your *mind*." I splayed my hands. "Stingray through the heart! Crazy, right?"

Smirking, incredulous: "You are such a dumbass." You started the engine. "That's yesterday's news."

Oh.

"Why'd you think I *said* that?" And you chuckled, shaking your greasy head.

I folded up the newspaper primly. "I thought we were making up cool deaths."

You laughed out loud, genuinely, and stuck the Fifty Foot Wave CD in, turned it all the way up. "Get the fuck outta my van," you yelled over the music. But you said it like it was a compliment.

So I did. I got the fuck outta your van and took it as a compliment. "See you in my dreams!" you snarled. And then you pulled away, dirt and dirty feathers flying.

This is when you started to hate me, I guess. Still don't know why, but this is *when*. You were hard to read. So much backstory and not just shooting trees and eating candy and not eating candy and drinking and driving and cracking your spine and flying around in the air on waves of sound. All the worlds of thought you didn't articulate, even to yourself. We all caught some, like glimpses of your reflection . . . maybe even some you missed. I mean, all your friends could see you pretty clearly and you'd always been a mystery to yourself. Then again, maybe we just *thought* we could see you clearly. Lies upon lies and lies back. Lie back for more lies.

But those reflective glimpses were adding up and they were petrifying, putrifying your future.

A mutual friend told me that your X-rays had once been presented to a class of medical students. When the professor asked them what movement they guessed the patient was capable of, what amount of control was left, the students had decided: nothing below the tongue.

Now, your tongue was capable of great feats of whiplash and destruction, of poetry and analysis, of cruelty, both justified and wholly cruel: cruelty for its own sake. But your flailing arms and twisting torso, your facile, fluttering, and frozen fingers pulling music out of the air, you driving yourself through Europe, navigating both its *strasses* and its stairs, you decking a waif with your explosive backhand, you leaning over an amplifier in frustration, searching for better toggles and switches. You reaching out to pet a coatimundi in Mexico, for christ sake.

I still don't know anybody who moves as much as you did. It's as if the rest of us don't bother, so we atrophy. Fighting, you remained a twisting dust devil to the end, impaling yourself and everybody else on whatever gear shift was handy. Filthy crust and a clean core, spinning out.

E-mails:

1/25

Hey, pal . . .

We have an offer on the table for west coast dates in early
spring, double bill, both of us together onstage again,
just fuckin' around, etc. Make your booking agent talk to
mine and we can play church again.

Love,

k

1/30

Vic?

My people wanna talk to yours and they want 'em to say
yes.

xo

k

2/10

Or no. Make them say *something*.

kisses,

k

2/15

Your voicemail is full and I'm tired of hearing it tell me
to fuck off, so just answer one of these goddamn e mails.
Type a letter. Any letter. Your favorite one. 26 to choose
from . . .

(Are you in Canada again?)

How 'bout we make that record together? You can try to sell out like you wanted, I don't care. In fact, I dare you. ponies,

k

2/20

Now we're getting worried. I mean we're actually worried. Seriously. Say something. Say anything except "fuck off."

Or say, "fuck off," I don't give a shit.

3/1

If you don't talk to me soon, I'm gonna sic Billy on you. He's from New York. He'll open up a can of city slicker whoop ass on you. Also? It's spring and we were gonna tour together, remember? SPRING. Flowers and hope and whatnot. All the things you hate. Baby bunnies. C'mon, dude.

3/15

There *is* a Vic Chesnutt, right? I mean, there was one *once*.

3/28

Nobody else knows where you are, either. If you were in another coma, you'd say so, right? I mean, you'd call?

4/25

Now I just call your cell because I *like* listening to you tell me to fuck off. Be better in person, though.

xo

p.s. Eat candy.

p.p.s. are you ok?

5/8

Remember how you told me that when we disappear, it's cuz we went to war?

Quit it.

love,

k

5/15

What the fuck, Vic? Now I'm pissed.

5/20

Not really, but you know what I mean.

5/30

James Victor.

Miss you.

Martha Kristin

Voice mails:

Vic? Kris. Call me.

Vic? Kris. Change your outgoing message. It was *almost* funny *once*. Now it's just juvenile. Also? Call me.

Vic? Kris. Tour is taken away. Off the table. So no pressure. We could just shoot the shit, cuz . . . what the hell is going on?

Vic? Kris. Call me. I called *you*. Now you call me *back*. Them's the rules.

Hello?

Vic? Kris. What the fuck. *Are* you in Canada again?

Vic? Kris. I actually want to talk. We're barely surviving as it is and now it looks like there's no more work. What're we gonna do? Could you call me and talk about what we're gonna do? We're already hungry. Soon we'll be dead. Or working fryolators. You got a hairnet? I don't.

Vic? Kris. I don't know what I did. But if you forgive me, we can move on and get back to work.

So we were no longer on speaking terms. Or I was and you weren't. With all your decency and secrets, you couldn't hide . . . what? I still don't know. Never will. Billy shrugged it off cuz he said it was to be expected, which was true. Bitch Chesnutt, etc. But still frustrating. Mostly because I'd assumed your ordinary orneriness was an act. So not special compared to the rest of you.

I had gathered that your friends were all supposed to take care of you, but I dunno. I wasn't good at it and Billy's point was a good one: we *couldn't*. "Not possible, not our responsibility," he assured me.

"It's messed up, though," I told him and he agreed. You didn't always act right.

Hating me was one of the times you died, but only the second one.

So I started listening to your records. I know you thought I *already* listened to your records, but I didn't really. I found facsimiles too "uncanny valley," the production obscuring, and I was snotty enough about the real you to prefer it.

But there was no real you anymore, so I started at the beginning and crawled through your years, measuring your time. Orgasms and mutations and unhappy accidents, like you said, but . . . more like small canvasses. You turned out to be much less violent than me. I mean, your reflections were so peaceful. Which was not how you wore them around us, certainly. But when you succeeded, it was because your songs told you what to do. That's true for everyone. I had a violent muse. She made me live scary stories so I could tell them.

But your muse was so *nice*. Even when she showed you your paper girl hanging from a tree, your muse was ice skating. When pigeons fell from your sky, she gave you doves: peace. Your songs told you to be gentle and I envied that. My throat hurt from all the yelling. My pigeons spun on tires.

People kissed gravel in my songs, ate their own skin. Chained to beds, they slept with dead people. Cravings led to mysterious packages on the front seat, blow jobs in the back. That's what love was to me. After a show, my guitar was blood-spattered. You? Became softer.

Tipping my umbrella forward just enough to make no eye contact with humans, I trudged mightily through the rain; fucked-up old leather boots splashing through torrential mud-pours, gray water swishing past the gutters, then up and over the sidewalk. Billy and I had lost just about everything: our house had filled with water and spat us out, then our work dried up. We were deeply in debt. So Portland, Oregon, took us in and helped us limp through a mushy, blurry winter of wondering . . . how. And goddamnit it why? Billy started a ticketing company that gave its proceeds to charity, giving when he had nothing. And Portland let me play shows; they showed up, made little fusses here and there, just kept me working. And kept me walking.

I could make eye contact only with dogs. And they stared back: blank, flat, dog depth. You played "Virginia" to me, sad and mad. "Virginia" is big and dramatic, of all things. *Drama? Seriously?* But yeah. Not melodrama, just the shit of wondering how and why, goddammit.

And crows staring down from rooftops and treetops. They must've been squawking, but I couldn't hear them. I only heard you listing the toxins that knocked you down once: *Vitalin, Vivarin, and Primatene, secret tequila shots, a patch of morphine.* The thump of your palm against the wood, pulling those nylon freakin' strings: *nylon? really?* But yeah. Nylon's what your grandfather played and you played your grandfather's guitar, so you played nylon strings. The only one of us who did, I bet. And you stretched those strings and worried them as you stretched and worried your list of poisons and regrets.

Sometimes I'd tip my umbrella up and a cone of swallows would tornado down this church chimney. Or maybe it was a school. Anyway, it was super weird. When it wasn't raining, Billy and I would park ourselves on the grass below and wait for the swallow tornado. People spread out blankets, opened bottles of wine, toddlers toddling. Then the swallows'd begin to fill the air above our heads—one bird at a time—and quiet became squeaky shrieking and the birds'd funnel and darken the sky, then scream down into the chimney and disappear. A breath of silence, then we'd all cheer, cuz what else do you do about a dark, shrieking funnel of birds? So we clapped.

And when I put my earbuds back in, you sang "Bakersfield." A man could retire on a melody like that, *should* be able to retire on a melody like that, anyway. You coulda leaned back, self-satisfied: finished. Hiding behind garbage cans, sainted. After death, a saint both exists and does not exist . . . so said the Buddha. "Bakersfield" is how I can understand that.

But you were an addict, so you didn't die yet. Addicted to hell's limo rides, you went and cliff-dove "Wrong Piano." Made us feel as nauseated as you, sickened by sound, like we didn't have enough to deal with already. Feigning sweetness, you dripped sugar, like you couldn't lie because you didn't know what lying was. Which was weird cuz you claimed to lie all the time. "I'm Through": *"forget everything I ever told you."* What *is* lying when it comes outta your mouth? *"I'm sure I lied way more than twice."* Like you're not sure.

"Crouched with a weak shovel" down "The Mysterious Tunnel" and up the dark, winding path in green, green, ultra-green Forest Park. Texted Billy as the sun that was never really there fell away behind enormous, mossy, bending trees, to tell him that orange salmon berries were winding around their trunks. Sent him a picture of cutthroat trout swimming up and downstream as you played "Arthur Murray" for Tina. A creepy bedtime story, a distant love song. Love song? Seriously? But yeah. A peeping tom's trouble is distant love and the noise you made was singing, so yeah. *"Emasculate me with your biology."* Love is always a little distant, unsure. We are all peeping tom's when it comes to the object of our affections. Forever troubled, forever shy.

I knew all these songs by heart, mind you. Right from your mouth, I knew where the palm thumps would fall, I knew the words. Sort of. When a song falls, it hits and when it *hits*, it . . . well, it's all encompassing. I never would have presumed to divide its concurrent pieces if I didn't have to. Like troubling, shy love, a song should just be.

But your records were sheet music; were like a distortion pedal, taken apart, dissected, its mysteries revealed. No, not *revealed*, cuz no cadaver'll help you with *how?* And goddammit *why?* But . . . I dissected your work that year. I'm sorry; I couldn't help it. Billy was falling, failing, my heart was on a wire, troubled and shy.

It rained so hard while Billy fell down into his own holes, became a black hole, a negative, a singularity, sucking me in. All I had left was my soundtrack and I hated it, preferred yours, as it was removed from the dark green fairy tale I was trudging through. And I had to dissect *something*. I don't know why, but I did. I guess because I wanted to understand something. A hole is nothing and Nothing is what haunted me.

Still stilled by Billy's shoulder, though, I leaned my head on a comfort I couldn't rescue from its darkness; I didn't know what else to do. I wanted substantive, so you stepped in and gave me some live song bodies to take apart, get ready for them to die.

But really, nobody's ever ready for anything to die.

Maladaptive malabsorption: if it goes in wrong, it's gonna come out wrong.

One morning, Billy said he had to die that day and then he walked out the door. Think about it: those two things don't go together. You don't *let* someone walk out the door if that's where they're going. The snapshot of his missing pieces flung itself off the motel nightstand in my amygdala, thrust in front of my eyes, my limbic system on fire. *This doesn't happen.* His holes had engulfed him, he was music without sound. And still beautiful, still mine. But his darkness was massive and I was so small. So thin, my ribs showed; so hunched from the rain, I lost inches of height and lung capacity. *How do I take care of him?*

This is when *it'll be okay* became *hold on*. Cuz how do you throw your arms around a black hole?

I didn't even try. I didn't grab him, didn't throw myself on the floor and block his exit; I couldn't move. Just froze, suddenly on the front lines and self-protective, of all things, then gone. Not in my body anymore. I heard my lips tell him to meet me on the corner near the drugstore at six; I guess cuz they thought if he was headed toward that corner, he couldn't walk out of hell and into heaven. At least not today. Billy gave me an odd look. My fucked-up lips kissed him and the look faded, then he turned his back on me and left.

How do you keep yourself from shattering? You don't. You take care of your loved ones. Every-fucking-body knows that. But frozen was how I lived through that day. Then, numb, I calmly walked to the drugstore, knowing that Billy wouldn't be there. Had I known how enormous my heart really was, how huge every cardiac moment really is, I could have wrapped everything I was around him and saved him. Cuz we are all essentially safe and strong. But I didn't know that then and neither did he.

Standing on the corner outside a glowing drugstore, I waited and waited. No Billy. I was frozen in a painting of waiting. Tried to stop imagining myself having thrown my weak little body on the floor and blocked his exit that morning, starting everything over, teaching him to breathe, breathing for him, marrying him again that afternoon. The afternoon which was now pink and fading, the sun that was never really there leaving for good.

It was getting dark. *Purple* and fading. Then slate. No Billy. I walked into the drugstore and began filling a shopping basket with pills, wondered if our maxed-out credit card would work. I had to look at my arm and will it to lift. *This doesn't happen.* I felt the panic rise into my chest and shoved it down, soothed by the image of swallowing all the pills in my basket. Just shove them all down, shove it all down.

No Tina was how you lived. Lived all of your days. I had barely peered down into your chasm and I was falling apart. How did you do it? There is no real word for heartbreak, our senses captured and released in a flood of their opposed responses: a negative of love's photograph.

My cell phone glowed green with an incoming text from a friend; glowed green next to the little plastic bottles with gentling blue names on them telling me to calm down, give in, fall asleep, it'll be okay, sleep. "GO OUTSIDE," said the text, "AND LOOK AT THE MOON." And I knew Billy had done it. How would you tell a wife that her husband had killed himself because she didn't throw her weak little body down on the floor and block his exit? Because she had done no pre-weeping, no funeral wailing for the benefit of the heart they shared that was *still beating* that morning? No breathing for both of them? No putting his oxygen mask on first and slipping into unconsciousness, happy that she saved him? Who freezes instead? Who goes numb when they should go crazy? A dead wife, that's who.

So you would tell this dead wife about her dead husband by telling her to go outside and look at the fucking moon. For a little grandeur and perspective and because you're chicken-shit scared that you'll cry if you tell her and she'll die if you tell her, so you'd send a moon text to buy yourself time.

And what did *I* do? I did what my friend told me to do. I

put down my basket of pills and went outside to look at the moon. I clapped for the swallows.

Don't remember really what the moon looked like that night. Probly big and yellow. Maybe big and white. I froze under it, just stood there, looking up. The moon did indeed buy my friend some time; it caught me off guard to have something to do. But how long can you stand there and look up, in a painting of waiting? Not too long if you have a short attention span and you aren't real evolved. *No Billy*.

My freeze choked and my hands started to shake. I turned to go back for my pills in the drugstore and saw Billy's silhouette. *Oh my god*. I crumpled as he walked up—so dark, so slow—and then leaned into his sad, angry, black hole chest and in one poison tear from each eye, wept out my funeral wailing. I was maybe a dying wife, and he was maybe a dying husband, and I hadn't helped or saved either of us, but I wrapped my arms around a black hole that was *still here, still mine*. I felt a sliver of the enormous heart we shared. And we weren't dead yet.

Thank you, god. Thank you.
Sometimes I think it's dumb that you were an atheist.

And why the fuck did my friend tell me to look at the moon?

Billy standing, I kept walking—*hold on*—Portland a green, urban, odd backdrop for your sound. I learned this, out in the silvery mist: don't look down at your feet, look up at the canopy above.

One night when the mist became rain and the rain became a waterfall, the path in Forest Park became rapids. Sad Peter Pan was singing "Sad Peter Pan": *when did I get perverted?* Which was interesting, caught my attention. I'm intrigued by the perversions that plague us, twisting simple urges into complex dis-ease.

So I *saw* the people running out of the woods when I was walking in, but it didn't really register that they might not be jogging but running away from something. Or that I didn't usually have to struggle so hard in order to move forward. My busted old boots were underwater, then my knees were, too, and my boots filled with muddy goo. "*I'm just pushing the paint around/on advice from your lying mouth,*" you sang, sounding sleepy. There were those lies again. According to you, we all just let our lips move. Which, I'll admit, resonated.

Suddenly, a man raced up to me in the dark, put an arm around my waist and spun me around, tugging me out of the path of a fallen tree that was rolling down the hill at us. I didn't know he was gonna do that, so I didn't have time to pull out my earbuds. I didn't yet know that the whole city was flooding, half our house underwater, the few belongings we'd rescued from our last flood floating in brown liquid. I couldn't hear this wet stranger yelling or the pounding rain; all I heard was you:

> All alone and awkward
> But a transformation
> I swear it will occur

All music ever gave anybody is a whole nuther world to hide in. A wholesome, dirty one, made of sailing off cliffs and when you land? The rocks below take you apart and fly you back up again in a split second, that you may live to sail off another cliff when the time is right: Prometheus fucked. Hopefully, you take somebody with you, somebody deserving or maybe even an asshole who needs his breath sucked away in an adrenaline rush.

Or maybe music tells you *you're* the asshole and you find out when life pictures flash before your eyes, in a goofy, lovely movie of a song. Even the shame of it is kind of . . . elegant. Or maybe just universal. Sweet, anyway, touching: Prometheus baptized. If eagles eat our livers, we can't fight off poison and shame is poison. But if you're ashamed, really, how big an asshole could you be? Not beyond saving.

Music: "So what were we afraid of all this time? So many of us, so terrified. Of what? Ourselves or each other?" *Pretty soon I know I'll do/Precisely what I wanted not to do.*

Either way, the math works. Sick of the magic, we just want the numbers to add up, so we can heave a sigh of relief, crumple up the graying paper covered in figures and eraser marks, pitch it to the floor. We just wanna be *relieved* of it. But those beautiful numbers, you can't help smiling about them. Elegant equations, lying among the dust bunnies.

Billy did his damnedest to take care of me, but all those junkie lumberjacks who gathered around you . . . well, what they were all protecting wasn't you. You were just the bottle. It was the genie inside they wanted. I'm truly sorry about that. Only Tina could have helped the man and she was gone.

My earbuds, soggy in the Portland wet, spat your smooth crackling into my ears. Sometimes the bottle played, sometimes the genie inside. Trying to take up space makes noise. Vic the bottle used to try. Vic the genie knew how to let go. Letting go creates a cavernous space of . . . well, space. Which is then filled with rubbery poetry, the alien nature you were waiting to reconnect with.

Hold on, but let go. Whenever you let go, you were good. And when you were good, you were great. And when you were great, it didn't matter that Vic the bottle hated me. Vic the genie very sweetly blew me away.

And day after day, Billy walked up that street. First, a tiny silhouette, a gray smudge, instantly recognizable as my husband. I mean, the size and coloration of an owl, with no distinguishing characteristics and yet I knew it was him, standing another day. Sometimes we wanna die. And sometimes we watch each other live through it. This is maybe all that saving anyone ever amounts to.

IV. FIRST, GIVE

My bandmates and I pulled our van up to the sidewalk in front of Carnegie Hall and unloaded gear in the morning sunshine. Not a ton of gear; we were using house equipment as part of a gala dealie honoring R.E.M., who'd played an important role in our youth. Nice guys, too. Unusually nice. I mean, it's unusual for musicians who're more famous than others to not be vaguely focused on the area over your shoulder when you talk to them. The R.E.M. guys look you in the eye.

It was an honor to be asked to participate in a celebration of a band that invented something and maintained its integrity for decades. But it was not a comfortable thing. Muffled by coats and old grime, we pushed past stagehands and other musicians, lifting our guitars at odd angles to try and get by, wishing we were somewhere else.

The green room was full of people we knew or had heard of and a bunch of strangers. Full of flowers and nervous and coffee and murmuring and sudden loud, cutting laughter. Full of . . . wishing you were somewhere that was more yours.

Because what this event did was point out the ambiguity of a path. Who gets safety? Who gets work? Who gets music taken away in the struggle to get basic needs met? In the Great Depression of the music business, we all suddenly began to care about those paths. We had always struggled for Meaning; now we began to struggle for Survival. It was becoming clear that some of us had taken on heavier jungles than others, and some had been left behind altogether. None of it seemed to have much or anything to do with music.

It was R.E.M.'s special day, though, and they were good guys and nobody wants to point out any inherent sadness in a gala dealie while it's going on. The earnest musicians who sat with styrofoam cups of coffee in that green room were a little melancholy and jumpy is all. Tired.

Nobody wants to point out inherent sadness in a gala dealie except *you*, that is. When you wheeled into that green room with a *fuck you all and everybody else* grin, you were love and hate. You could do both at the same time! Plus: *it's all just a joke, so fuck it*.

It was funny and funny was what was missing. *Duh-uh*. My whiny internal rant seemed so goofy next to your goofiness, cuz you took it all on, while I just fussed inside. Plus, you can smell internal rants with a ten-foot pole, of course. Especially the pathetic ones. I shut up inside and you opened your arms, dousing every unanswered voice and e-mail I'd sent out into the ether that year in a spray of goodwill.

When I bent down to hug you, you said into my ear, "Fun party!" And I laughed, relieved of the burden of that hurtful, hateful year of silence. Where we were? Was not a fun party.

"Fun Party" was the dumbest, loudest, most excellent song in your catalogue; a drunken, impromptu recording of a goofy jam session in your attic that should never have happened, much less been captured on tape. Except, we were all so glad it was.

Sometimes I'd call you just to leave you a "Fuck you for 'Fun Party'" message. The worst earworm of all time, it was a killer foray into what it means to be annoying. Once, you told Billy you loved "Fun Party" so much, you actually took the time to re-cut the vocals, get 'em exactly right. Billy: "Vic's priorities are in upside down and backwards and right on target."

So at least three of us were breathing. *Now we move on.* I can move on. I'm good at moving on, great at moving on. It's like running away but nobody gets mad at you. In fact, you get Zen points for moving on because it looks so in the moment. I just couldn't stop smiling: the end of whatever-the-fuck *that* was. I didn't care what it was, didn't want to know. You weren't nuts anymore. You were clear and we had you back and that was all that mattered. You were probly just being a moody son of a bitch for a whole goddamn year. No surprises there. *Now we just need Tina to close the circle and none of us'll be lonely anymore.*

I remember it like this: you sleek, sashaying into the room, waving a big sword around, your no-bullshit sword. *Fuck you all and everybody else.* How could I have forgotten? Music wins, humility triumphs, the poor and broken seize the day. How *had* I forgotten? The only math that ever worked was that craziness and it was . . . simple. No sliding into obscurity when music is at your side. You aren't even *allowed* to slide; we have work to do. "The weak shall inherit the worth," you said, but only if they present as such. Both weak and worthy.

"*Shameful hollows, icy blue . . .*" you sang as you drew on the pristine, white wall with a Sharpie, "*. . . eyes/Spits or swallows, which do you?*" You finished your picture and capped the Sharpie. "Lies," you finished, hitting, what? Middle D? *Christ.* The period at the end of your sentence was always "lies."

I watched as you took out your cell phone, started hammering on it with your driving glove hand. "Who're you calling?"

You looked up at me, then gestured toward the monitor which showed us green room people what was happening onstage. R.E.M. was sound-checking, Michael Stipe standing bent, as if in prayer, near the microphone. "Him," you said offhandedly.

I looked up at the monitor, saw Michael take his cell phone out of his pocket and look at it as you hung up.

"They got faggoty food?" you asked me.

"Yeah, some. The caterer's vegan. But it's been picked over, just so you know."

Squint. "What do you mean, 'picked over'?"

"I mean . . ." lowering my voice, "*free food. You know. Some of these people are pretty poor. It's been picked over.*"

"HUMMUS IN PURSES?!" you shouted. The people around us jumped. Suddenly, your real voice came outta your mouth, freaky, like a possession: "*Pretty soon I know I'll do-o-o,*" you sang and I froze. "Hot Seat." "*Precisely what I wanted not to do-o-o . . . .*"

You remembered the line that haunted me most. I used to wake up in motel rooms, still sweaty from last night's show, burning with pre-hangover, hoping against hope that there was such a thing as hope. And that's what I would hear: you singing, *"Pretty soon I know I'll do/Precisely what I wanted not to do."* You remembered. I stared at you, stunned.

"As far as harbingers go," you muttered, shaking your head sadly, "that's not a good one." A coupla shattering blue portals. "Hope you been containing your excesses."

Most people who know me would not associate me with excesses of any kind, but you knew better. You gave me a flat dog-depth stare, then moved on. "If the hummus has been PICKED OVER!" you announced, glaring around the room suspiciously, "we should maybe order in!"

"Vic?" I couldn't help it. "How's Tina?"

"Aaaaah . . . we're Archie and Edith Bunker."

I didn't know what this meant, but maybe neither did you. "Does that mean you're . . . together?" Our diner scene came back in a rush of midwestern snow. The four of us *not alone.*

"We couldn't afford a divorce after all. Those things are *expensive.*" Your eye caught mine. "You ever priced 'em?"

"*No.*" I shook my head and you shrugged off any more conversation. *There'll be time to ask questions later.*

My bandmates and I watched you perform from side of stage that night. You looked . . . like a well-rested hick, like you were wheeling out to the back porch to shell peas or something. Incongruous in Carnegie Hall. Even when New Yorkers try to dress down they look dressed up, because they did it on purpose. You radiated a rumpled focus that nobody could imitate. Except maybe somebody waking up on the sidewalk in a good mood and that almost never happens.

A sunshiny Polaroid appeared in my head: us on that Spanish sidewalk with Billy and Tina, everyone staring. And here we were in New York, everybody still staring at you. *At least they're paying attention*, I thought.

We were all playing R.E.M. covers that night; it was a celebration of R.E.M. after all, so none of us felt real secure in what we were doing. I could tell *you* didn't, but your face had that look you get when you have a secret. I mean, a good secret; not secret tequila shots or secret airport men's room floor pills.

Your secret turned out to be that you could play R.E.M. covers and sweep the floor with the rest of us. We were all sort of getting by, getting through the night, feeling less-than and lowly. You? Killed us. "Everybody Hurts" and in your hands, it rang heartlessly true. *You can play covers? Without sounding lame?* But yeah, cuz it's not like you invented any of the other chords you played or the words you zapped with your alchemy to turn them into your lyrics. It was a twisted thing that you brought to the table. Popping open the genie bottle, you twisted someone else's song; kept twisting and twisting until you'd wrung every tear out of it and us.

I hugged you when you came off stage, looking so smug. "You win," I told you, like you didn't already know that, but I knew how badly you wanted to hear it.

Holding bottles of beer and cups of tea with my bandmates and the other musicians, we stared up at the monitor. Having made this green green room a little funnier, we'd relaxed enough that our laughter was now genuine. Success is real music, failure is sucking. That's all, no biggie. We were maybe a loser club and this was maybe one of our loser clubhouses, but none of us had actually *failed*.

R.E.M.'s encore with Patti Smith played fuzzily across the monitor. She'd forgotten the words and sort of fits-and-starting stopped the song halfway through. We all watched as the R.E.M. guys quit playing their parts, one at a time. "Did they just . . . stop?" someone asked.

I tilted my head to the side, trying to understand the monitor from a better angle. "I didn't know we were allowed to do that."

When the song started up again, Michael fell to his knees and bowed to Patti, the way he'd bowed to the mic stand during soundcheck. You immediately took out your cell phone. I stared, wide-eyed. "Vic, you're not calling Michael again?"

"Nope."

"Good."

You pounded your driving glove fist into the phone. "Texting him."

I laughed and squinted down at the tiny screen over your shoulder. You had, of course, written: "YOU SUCK. LOVE, VIC."

At the aftershow, you told me it was time to say good-bye. I looked at my watch. "It's only eleven."

After R.E.M. tribute, March 11, 2009. The last time I saw Vic. Photo by Chris Owyoung.

Shrugging. "Yeah, but still." Stare. I took a minute to look you over, check your vitals. Your lips had thinned, but your skin still glowed. And maybe Tina was back for real; I'd know soon. Smiling, I hugged you. "Okay. Be careful out there. Call me about studio time. We'll tour whatever we record. Send me demos."

"Right on," you grinned, and waved over your head as you sped out the door. The wave became hailing a cab as you disappeared into the bright, glary New York version of night.

The third time you died, they said it was just another coma. We were living in New Orleans, party town for the partied down—a city-wide Fun Party to keep the citizens occupied, but also a ship of lost souls. Our souls weren't lost, just dangling, but we'd seen firsthand how easily a body can wander off. Wandering was all around us.

DON'T SUCK, DON'T DIE

Billy called from the grocery store a few days before Christmas and said you were in the hospital again, hadn't heard much else. OD'd on muscle relaxants. *Oh god, not again. Poor Tina.*

So I called around to see what we all thought about this one. Stared out my window at elephant ears and palms, at our dogs panting on the porch, waiting for our friends to answer their phones. Somebody said you looked real good, nice color, just out cold. Somebody else said you were about to talk, they could tell. Except you were gonna be so pissed off when you opened your eyes, they didn't wanna be there to hear what you had to say. Tina wasn't answering her phone.

But we figured, all of us together, we could wake you up out of a *coma*, for christ sake. Easy. Those happened all the time: *Vitalin, Vivarin, and Primatene/secret tequila shots and a patch of morphine.* We just needed the anti-venom for all that poison. Billy also said, "Be ready," though. I took a deep breath cuz I didn't expect him to say this. I mean, I was practically rolling my eyes about another goddamn coma but he thought this one we should maybe take seriously. Don't know what it was that sobered him; maybe New Orleans teaching us fragile. Maybe life knocking him down enough that he was only half-standing, unsure. Maybe just knowing you and your efforts to leave this plane.

Muscle relaxants, though? So tame for you. A grandma'd go that way. *I'd* go that way. So nah, that wouldn't do it. Stingray through the heart, death by quagga, mystery microbe, suit of armor on a golf course in an electrical storm. *Billy's just trying to take care of me.*

And the crazy will that made your limbs flail and your guitar play wasn't gonna let you lie around in a hospital bed for too long. You loved it here. In my opinion, you were talking shit when you said you were an atheist. I don't know what you thought God was, but there was nobody more worshipful than you. You must've known this, felt weakened by it, so you said "atheist" about yourself and your friends believed you and journalists wrote it down . . . but godliness was your shameful secret and you knew it. Speed Racer, my ass. You prayed constantly, worshipped everything, infused with the spirit to the point of speaking in tongues. Coma . . . gimme a break. So I hugged Billy cuz he was worried about me and told him that as soon as Christmas was over, I was going to Athens to wake you up.

Cuz it was *Christmas*, after all, so, yeah: Fun Party. Get up. Get up and then it'll be a fun party. *Merry Christmas, Vic! Get off your ass and get back to work.*

Honestly? I didn't feel like I even *knew* you anymore. But these were the notes left on my amygdala's nightstand. Billy: "Be ready." And you: "I wanna be a ghewst."

Christmas morning. A mutual friend booked me a commuter flight from New Orleans to Atlanta, said he'd pick me up at the airport and bring me to the hospital in a few days. Tina'd be there, hurting but keeping you safe, as always. And you'd count her braids down to nothing by just waking-the-fuck-up. We'd have dozens of friends there, taking turns watching you lie around, letting machines breathe for you. People hardly ever cried over you, I already knew that; cuz you liked laughter so much. Gravity is a given, it doesn't ask for tears.

I was thinking I might even sneak tequila into the hospital and I was definitely bringing you this new song where I thought I might've ripped you off for a minute. Inadvertently, but I knew your ego bubble'd enjoy that. In the outro was this section where I doubled the acoustic leads and they mingled in an unusually layered fashion you'd immediately recognize as one of your trademark moments. I always pretended I didn't know how to do it, but really I just didn't wanna be *caught* doing it. And I did it anyway, by accident. The timing even got fluid after that, just like yours, when the busy-ness of sound fell away and the thickness of a lacuna took over, so the words hung heavy. The whole section was kinda . . . uh . . . mushy. I can't think of a better word. You'd call it esoteric or imagistic and I'd snicker when you did. Anyway, it reminded me of that dream song of yours floating out over the lake in Madison.

Standing in my closet, I shoved a CD of that song into my backpack with a book and a dress and my cell phone. As I did, the phone rang. It was our friend who'd bought my plane ticket to Georgia so we could wake you up together. I knew he was calling to wish us a merry Christmas, but hopefully, he was also gonna tell me my plane tickets were squared away and you were on liquids and home for the holiday. Then it'd snow . . .

I fished around in my backpack and found the vibrating phone. *It will so totally snow, I know it. And clean, southern snow will be magic and cool. It'll wake you up like in the Wizard of Oz. Cuz it's only poppies that ever knocked you out in the first* place. Snow would be the anti-venom. Billy would love that; he was such a snow guy. Used to go to football games in the snow, be the only one sitting in the bleachers. We'd challenge each other to walk across town on winter nights, slipping on the ice, trudging over unshoveled sidewalks. Maybe I never told you about that. Now's my chance, you trapped in bed and bored, snow falling outside the hospital window.

Snow in Georgia on Christmas'll make your friends laugh and when you open your eyes and start yelling at 'em, then yeah, maybe some of them *will* cry, gravity be damned. And sparkly white and quiet'll be the story we tell about this coma. *You and your comas, for christ sake, you need a new hobby. This one's gettin' old.*

"Merry Christmas," I hummed into the phone and tossed a nicer pair of shoes into my backpack in case you were eating solid food by the time I got there and we ended up going to dinner somewhere other than the Grit. Unlikely, since you refused to go anywhere other than the Grit. Even though once they served you a carrot on a hot dog bun and called it a "veggie dog." You were pretty pissed off about that. That bewildered eye-roll of yours that meant: "everybody is a dumb ass and so are the dumbasses who write the books they read and so are the dumbasses that play the music they listen to and plus, look at this goddamn hot dog bun with a goddamn carrot stickin' out of it."

"I'm packing, so I hope you got me that plane ticket or I'll be riding on the wing," I muttered, looking at my gross thrift shop clothes in the dark closet. "Oh, do you think I have to look nice or can we just porch-hang? Or is he still gonna be in the hospital? And can I look shitty in the hospital?"

You ate that carrot dog anyway, as mad as you were, which just goes to show you what a good sport'll do: slather lime pickle all over food and down it. With an instant coffee chaser. *Christ.*

Our friend was crying. "He's gone."

I dropped the backpack on the floor and sat down on it. "Oh." *Tina, go outside and look at the moon.* The wall tilted to the left. When I stood up to touch it, *I* tilted to the left, too, so I sat down again. *Where's Billy?* My phone was still vibrating, as if I hadn't answered it. It was freezing in that closet. I tried to leave the cold closet, but I was too sideways, so I went back in. *Where's Billy?*

Our friend broke down and sobbed. I sat in the dark closet on my backpack, listening to him cry. The lightbulb had been burned out in this closet since we first rented the place. Billy could fix anything; how come he hadn't changed the lightbulb? Billy could fix *anything.*

Maybe I started to cry then, I don't know. "I love you," our friend choked, and hung up.

In the diner with the little orange-yolked eggs, Tina lifted her fork and studied her reflection, touched her brown curls. "Too many tines," I told her. "Use the knife." When she lifted her butter knife, you told her to put it down, that she looked beautiful and looking wasn't gonna make her any more beautiful. You told Tina that looking at her was your job, not hers. This was how you took care of your wife: in knife blades.

I need a black dress.

It really isn't possible that some quiet Big Bang in a hospital room could reverse itself and suck all that was Vic Chesnutt back into nothingness. Or whatever the hell you were or were not now. Speed Racer. *Merry goddamn Christmas, Vic.*

No, sorry, didn't mean that.

But dead? Like, dead forever? That is so . . . not fun. Everything used to be fun. That's how I remember it, anyway. Breathless, exhilarated, hungry. As systemically sad as we were. Actually maybe because of the sadness. Tina laughing and putting her butter knife down because you loved her. Billy, easy, calling himself evil and ugly because I loved *him*. Our whole world was goofy as shit. Little Kinder Surprise toys flying over the heads of hypocrites, thumbtacks pressed into the hammers of a pretentious piano. It was dark and we were dirty, there were bugs all over our ceiling, skull quadrants floating in oily coffee, three-legged dogs who wouldn't love us, and we hardly ever stopped laughing. I mean, why would you? I guess when there isn't anything to laugh at anymore.

No more pain for you, maybe. You'd won the race to the finish, but what were *we* supposed to do? All us other mutants and aliens, confused and lonely again. You'd made mutations look so good.

I couldn't think of anything to do except carry your body through the streets. I tweeted that you were gone, of all things; told thousands of people. I typed a bunch of letters into my phone and I suppose a kind of wail went up.

Billy could fix anything except he couldn't. He did remind me that we had to help Tina. *Right*. Helping Tina seemed like the rightest, proactivest, kindest, make-it-all-okay-againest thing we could do. *Okay. Help Tina.*

I blinked up at him. "How?"

"Ask people to give." Billy's eyes were red and red-rimmed.

Me, not thinking straight: "Give?"

". . . Tina money. To cover medical costs, help her pay her mortgage."

Right. Help Tina. I wished I had told Tina to go outside and look at the moon, but now it was too late. She wasn't answering her phone, anyway.

So I sat in front of the computer for hours, staring at a bright, dead screen. Bright and dead like you. I wanted to reach for Billy's hand, but he wasn't there. He'd left me alone with my thoughts. The room I was in was enormous; a big New Orleans parlor back in the day, I guess. Now it was empty except for a table, a mess of paper, a computer, and me. And you were there, too, floating around.

There was this big Vic, like a burst of weather in the room. A giant, invisible bird or a disease. Some kind of you was happening while I stared at that screen instead of crying on Billy's shoulder. I wanted to feel sorry for myself, *did* feel sorry for myself, but Billy knew we had to feel sorry for Tina first.

And the new Vic: the weather/bird/germ, was so happy. You were a free thing, undamaged, clean. You were a glistening listening, a giant smile with pristine, glossy wings, no more shame. A Vic who isn't angry? What the hell is that?

This was the first time "win" didn't mean "lose." You were finally a drunken angel, clean from heaven's ablutions, just like Hank Williams. *You* were still laughing.

I smiled for a second, then, stunned by the smile, cried. "What are you smiling about?" I asked you, my voice a shaky echo in the empty room. But it was you, alright. You had done something brave. Possibly a terrible, brave *mistake*, but you wanted out and you got out, took Christmas with you. A surprise ending that surprised no one.

I'd thought you'd have to earn back your wings one feather at a time, since you were a kind of anti-Icarus, sweeping the floor of hell with them. But, no, you got 'em back in a decadent night of muscle relaxants and darkness. Oh how we'd all loved that darkness.

Your bodyless self helped that Christmas night because it was like lighting a fire. Nothing more, nothing less, than a hearth on which to focus before I buried my face in Billy's chest. When you are paralyzed because another alien on earth just flew away, you sorta need a focus other than "huh?" And your ghewst very kindly provided a bit of warmth to combat the "huh?"

Though I still feel a little of it when I reach for the phone to call you and remember you don't have a phone anymore, when I listen to a song of yours and the vocals are mixed so loud that you sound close by. Friend, asshole, angel, mutant, it's easy to forget you left. But, you know . . . it is what it is. Anyway, this is what I wrote about the substantive nothing you had become:

What this man was capable of was super human. Vic was brilliant, hilarious and necessary; his songs messages from the ether, uncensored. He developed a guitar style that allowed him to play bass, rhythm and lead in the same song—this with the use of only two fingers. His fluid timing was inimitable, his poetry untainted by influences. He was my best friend.

I never saw the wheelchair—it was invisible to me—but he did. When our dressing room was up a flight of stairs, he'd casually tell me he'd meet me in the bar. When we both contracted the same illness, I told him it was the worst pain I'd ever felt. "I don't feel pain," he said. Of course. I'd forgotten. When I asked him to take a walk down the rain spattered sidewalk with me, he said his hands would get wet. Sitting on stage with him, I would request a song and he'd flip me off, which meant, "this finger won't work today." I saw him as unassailable—huge and wonderful—but I think Vic saw Vic as small, broken. And sad.

I don't know if I'll ever be able to listen to his music again, but I know how vital it is that others hear it. When I got the phone call I'd been dreading for the last fifteen years, I lost my balance. My whole being shifted to the left; I couldn't stand up without careening into the wall and I was freezing cold. I don't think I like this planet without Vic; I swore I'd never live here without him. But what he left here was the sound of a life that pushed against its constraints, as all lives should. It's the sound of someone on fire. It makes this planet better.

And if I'm honest with myself, I still feel like he's here, but free of his constraints. Maybe now he really is huge. Unbroken. And happy.

I called you my best friend because you'd seen The Singer who haunted us, but, like I said, I didn't really know you anymore. Not the man or the weather-bird. You were out-of-the-corner-of-my-eye, like a floater or a story. That's it: you'd become a story. Not a bad thing at all.

Friends, loved ones, musicians, and people none of us knew sent dollar after amazing dollar to help Tina because Billy knew we weren't allowed to feel sorry for ourselves until enough care was scattered around. And we gave your woman as much as *we* had, too, which wasn't that much, but it was doing something.

Then you can freeze and your knees are allowed to knock and you can shiver sideways and fall on each other. Then the tears are allowed to fall and you bury yourself in your favorite chest, on your favorite shoulder. But first, give.

Your house looked the same. I didn't understand how you could have left before all your lentils were gone; kept staring at the half-full jar. I figured if you had some lentils left, you must be coming back. Like you just popped out to heaven, were gonna come back with maybe some tomatoes and cumin.

Stared out your window. Our window in your house, really. Same view at the foot of our futon. I saw Billy hungover under the flowered sheets. Remembered calling us road hogs cuz we were always crashing at your place and you'd said all road hogs were road warriors. You wrote a little poem about us blessing your house with our sweaty, road warrior selves, when you knew all that you meant to us homeless hogs. Billy and I were the hog children, not y'all. *We* were the needy homeless. We'd stared out that window so many times, happy to be off the road a minute, safe in our Safe House. So happy that Billy tried to move us next door once: to the dusty, hair-sprayed woman's house. Thirty birds in her kitchen and at least that many rats in her attic. So happy. *What am I now, sad? Numb?*

Guess if I don't know, then I'm numb. I must've looked sad though, cuz someone hugged me. Someone I didn't know. Or didn't remember.

People kept giving me coffee, so I'd hold a cup for a while and then put it down somewhere. Then someone else'd give me coffee. More people came. Somebody I *did* know hugged me. Now your house was filling up with people. Most of them looked like junkie lumberjacks. God, were you loved. That flimsy ego, that giant bubble we could pop with one finger, when you were so admired and adored. Just crazy. You were just crazy.

My funeral shoes were killing me. They clicked across the wooden floor and stopped in front of your curio cabinet, filled with toys and crap. *Hey. A Steve Austin.* And it was Steve Austin, not Lee Majors, cuz he was dressed as the Six Million Dollar Man. When a face appeared in the glass behind my re-flection, I turned around, and Tina's father quietly introduced himself. "You're Kristin, right?" We hugged and I asked how

Tina was. He just held out his hands and started crying, so I hugged him again. He said he was grateful for the time they'd spent with you. *I'm glad you knew enough to treat Tina's parents right.*

Tina appeared in the door of a bedroom, looking . . . like Tina. Not divorced, not widowed, just grounded and glowing like she always did. Then she looked across the room and into my eyes and her lovely face screwed up, flushed dark red. Suddenly, she looked divorced, widowed, all of it. She broke down as she crossed the room and we hugged for . . . well, I guess a part of me feels like we're still standing there in your house, hugging. Needed by Tina was an honor. We fell on each other like marathon dancers, holding each other up, neither one of us supporting the other. Just floating together like gay hover truckers.

"Do you know how much he loved you?" she asked into my ear.

That diner morning again, the one with the real chicken eggs. Remembered the four of us as we were, laughing at coatimundis. It should be an old, used-up story that we move away from innocence, degraded by tragedies. I'm sick of it. Sick of reinventing it, sick of living it. "I want to go back in time," I told Tina and she nodded as tears ran down her cheeks. *Nobody should make Tina cry*, I thought. *Not even you.*

Grief can feel selfish—or at least self-absorbed—but grief for a suicide, less so. There is an element of sorrowful anguish you don't feel in other deaths when someone takes their own life. A pity. What a pity. You feel so. Much. Pity. The driver at fault in a car accident is the last one to have been able to prevent the accident. What was your last thought? The one that could have prevented this accident? We all blame it for your death and none of us will ever know what it was. I pitied you your brain and its commands.

And I pitied those of us who imagined they could have stepped out in front of it and saved you from the muscle relaxants which relaxed you out of your self, like hard Tina's hard sleeping pills. Good thing you were hard, too. Were those muscle relaxants sugarcoated at least?

"We have to take care of people like you," Tina whispered and I faced her, shaking my head. "We have to take care of people like *you*," I told her. "Vic was broken. This is not your fault." Thank god Tina belongs somewhere. Thank god she has a home.

Her pink, tear-stained face paused and she took me by the arm, leading me into the hallway outside your bedroom. "Would you like some time alone with him?"

I stopped in front of your bedroom door and looked into her steady brown eyes. "I don't think I can do this."

"You can," she answered lightly, as if I'd told her I couldn't open a can of soup. "You'll see."

As she walked away, I noticed that her graying hair was combed through; no braids. This was a no-braids day for Tina.

Alone in your room, I sat on the bed with your remains. In the corner was your empty wheelchair and your guitar, your clothes hanging in the closet. It felt like it used to except . . . you were dead. I don't actually remember you being there. Not like when you were flying around my parlor. It was real empty in your bedroom that morning.

I had a cinnamon Jolly Rancher in my purse. Bought a bag at the Atlanta airport and pitched all but one. Figured I'd trade it for a guitar pick, but I didn't see any picks around, so I just left it on your pillow. "Eat candy, dammit," I said out loud and then felt stupid. Too late to send you gentle into any good night, anyway. "See you in my dreams," I tried and it sounded even dumber. I hoped that there was no one listening outside the door trying to make up their own last words to you.

I really didn't know what to do. *Still don't know how to pray. Better get on that.*

So I looked out the window instead of at what they told me was you now. I wanted to be a good friend, but you weren't saying anything and you wouldn't, not ever again. Oddly, out the window, though, there was . . . peace. Georgia peace. I thought I'd made that up. When it came to you, I was empty and emptiness was perfect. Doesn't sound like me to be that Zen, but there it is. I used to know you and that's all. Dying makes people seem important, and that's too much responsibility for a soul that's no more or less than any other. I guess you had enough mojo left on this plane to carry some heaven over to the window and smear it on the glass. Thanks for that.

I didn't cry too much about you. You were and then you weren't. I mean, you happened and then you didn't. Billy was my shoulder and I was his and all the sadness in our lives was quiet, always. Between the two of us, it came and went. Our sadness for *you* came and went. Not sure it got to you up there skimming the ether, finally eclipsed by sound.

V. SEE YOU IN MY DREAMS

A mosquito can fell a broken heart.

When Billy's hammer came down, almost a quarter of a century into the game, there wasn't a blindfold in sight. Still, I didn't see it coming, and right before it hit me, I thought it might whistle past, a glancing blow or something. But no, it was aimed at me, it blew my soul outta my ears. They didn't save us, Vic . . . we broke *them*.

Those heroes you men were? They were the angels. Cuz hearts are hard and you carried 'em in your chests anyway. Carried ours too. Tina and I were swept along by that . . . slept through it almost, it was such a dream.

At your memorial service, I was asked when I was gonna get mad at you. "Never," I answered. And I meant it. I never loved you. But your Tina? I dunno, I imagine she will always be angry. That's gonna have to be your hell in heaven, I guess. You'll drop a few feathers over that one.

I've been to heaven. It had a view. On the outside, through the windshield, but on the inside, too.

Heaven was a jumble of senses. Seeing it was feeling it, proprioceptors kept our hearing balanced, our skin hungry. Color-saturated bloodstreams're infused with roadrunners and shaky blue cans there. Heaven had us shaking off our selves so we could live for each other. It had a lousy gray beach, clouds around its apartment building, static electricity and the ghost of a Ferris wheel. The stories don't stop in heaven because its clock keeps no time up there on the mantel over the fireplace, in hazy black and white, looking down on armchairs full of friends and lovers. I can see us so clearly there.

Had the devil not stepped in and fucked with our lovely limbo, kicking us downstairs, we'd still be there. As piercing as it is, as excruciating its injury, hell is boring. The weird part is the suddenness of the tumble. I imagine all Satan's gotta do is snap an eyepatch over your good eye and then, blind, you fall from grace.

But . . . I wonder if grace is patient. You know, hazy and forgiving. I wonder if she keeps no score and no time. I mean, heaven isn't going anywhere.

I'm the only one of the four of us still living our life. I still go to scuzzy church, still stare out over our drunken congregation and make 'em listen. Music still happens between me and those faces. I go to truckstops and wish the truckers'd just fall in love, goddamn it. My dressing rooms are empty but for me and my guitar and a Sharpie. And the lipstick I use to draw new lips on over my crooked ones.

The Mint, Los Angeles, 2000. Photo
by Kerina and Michael Marcon.

I'm alone backstage, then I'm alone *on* stage. Sometimes I
laugh, telling the stories that used to crack us up, sometimes I
wipe away tears while I pretend to reach for a drink or my set
list. Cuz music hurts so goddamn much, always did. Sometimes I do nothing but let songs disappear me. I shake off my
body and my soul and go away and that's the best. When I feel
absolutely nothing.

I did finally learn how to pray: you ache with a hope that
sifts through your skin, down into your muscle memories and
through your nervous nerves and beating vitals, until your
skeleton is pressed into a compression, into a singularity. Not
an abyss but a comfort of a black hole, into nothing at all.
Then hope is gone and so are you.

Heaven and earth are impartial.
They allow all things to die.
    Lao Tzu

Everything dies. Love, even. Good-bye, Billy.
You, even. Good-bye, Vic.
See you in my dreams.

SELECTED DISCOGRAPHY

Little (1990) opens the door to a musical world the way a debut album should: swinging wide, elaborately revealing every idiosyncratic detail Vic would wear on his sleeve throughout the rest of his career. Spindly, percussive conversation rather than traditional lyrics, spider web guitar and a grasp of melody both complex and irresistible, songs like "Rabbit Box" and "Bakersfield" capture the childlike, bitter soul that was Vic at his best.

West of Rome (1991) finds a brokenhearted Vic "crying in his hummus" ("Where Were You?"), singing a love song to the state of Florida, "the redneck Riviera" ("Florida"), and building a memory out of sparklers and darkness that we make our own then can't forget: "*My earliest memory/is of holdin' up a sparkler/high up to the darkest sky*" ("Panic Pure"). It's a walk around a landscape suffused with humid southern air and Vic's sharpened sense of dream as reality.

Is the Actor Happy? (1995) is a brilliantly executed work of outstanding material, both crashing and delicate. No listener, no matter how unfamiliar with the language Vic spoke, could walk away from songs like "Thailand," "Wrong Piano," and "Sad Peter Pan." *Is the Actor Happy?* never wavers from its power to grab, assault, and wheedle, celebrating both goofiness and trauma. As hard as Vic could be as a songwriter, as a singer, he was always kind and this gentle enthusiasm informs every track here.

About to Choke (1996), the first record Vic made for Capitol, has a few anthemic choruses and some hooks, of all things, but opens with "Myrtle," a quiet, heartbreaking work of exceptional gravity. "Hot Seat" is a confoundingly universal list of all that made Vic tick and everything that ultimately undid him. How is that universal? You got me, but it resonates and we relate, whether we want to or not.

The Salesman and Bernadette (1998) was a kind of concept album, though that reductionist take is not how this record leaves you. Vic portrays himself as a homesick traveling salesman, in love with his faraway wife. Apt description of a touring musician, but these songs are so peaceful, so elegant and smooth with Lambchop as his backing band, that the story rises above itself. The rolling nature of a human being—the driving, wandering gypsies that we are—is shown as not a restlessness but a culmination of impulses. Finally in "Arthur Murray," it's revealed to be a dance.

Ghetto Bells (2005) was Vic at his biggest. *Ghetto Bells* feels tragic. The production is itself so respectful of the work, this record can be hard to listen to unless you're ready to be moved. There is nothing gentle about "Virginia," its overwhelming drama and string section crying along with Vic that love makes us die. "To Be with You" is equally heartbreaking and not necessarily a ride we want to take with the man that infused most of his other work with humor and a light touch. Dark magic is still magic, though, and heavy with caring. A body of work without the weight of this record would have felt unfinished.

Skitter on Take-Off (2009), Vic's last record, is a dissipation of sorts, but still lovely in that. He never wavered in his texture or delivery, which is where his real power lay. You can hear, close up, those bendy guitar strings and that whiny, grimy voice on "Feast in the Time of Plague" and "My New Life," but his muscles were giving out, giving up . . . I dunno, something is different. Not weak, just unfocused. It's a testament to Vic's character that that lack of focus reveals itself with such beauty here, such resonance. A necessary, essential shattering.

Vic's last show, Austin, Texas, 2009.
Photo by Sandy Carson.